C000178863

Illustrated Dictionary of
Sailing Ships, Boats and Steamers
1300 BC to 1900 AD

ILLUSTRATED DICTIONARY OF SAILING SHIPS, BOATS AND STEAMERS

Scott Robertson

ERRATUM

Page 117. Key to Illustration
1. Launch
2. Yawl
3. Pinnace
4. Cutter
5. Whaler

Page 45. Second drawing; XEBEC
Page 76. Abbreviation should read; RNLI
Page 139. Item 11; KLIPPER
Page 142. Last item; First steam lifeboat 1889

Nexus Special Interests, Nexus House, Azalea Drive, Swanley, Kent BR8 8HU

Illustrated Dictionary of Sailing Ships, Boats and Steamers 1300 BC to 1900 AD

Scott Robertson

NEXUS
SPECIAL INTERESTS

Nexus Special Interests Ltd
Nexus House
Azalea Drive
Swanley
Kent BR8 8HU

First published 2000

©Scott Robertson

The right of Scott Robertson to be identified as the Author of this work
has been asserted by him in accordance with the Copyright, Designs and
Patents Right Act of 1988.

All illustrations and diagrams appearing in this book have been originated
by the author except where otherwise indicated.

All rights reserved. No part of this book may be reproduced in any form
by print, photography, microfilm or any other means without written
permission from the publisher.

ISBN 1-85486-202-2

Printed in Great Britain by Whitstable Litho Ltd, Whitstable, Kent

Acknowledgements

The majority of illustrations have been originated by the author except where otherwise indicated.

Note Every effort has been made to trace, where necessary, copyright holders and to obtain permission for the use of copyright material and as references for preparing illustrations. My grateful thanks are due to the following:

Mike Bensley for his watercolour paintings from his book on Norfolk's past, including the cover picture to this book.

Elaine Ramsay of N.Z. Postcards, Christchurch, New Zealand.

Ian Allan Publishing, British Sailing Warships.

Mike Cannings, SS 'Great Britain' Project.

Jonathan F Eaton of International Marine, Rockport, USA with reference to American Sailing Craft by H I Chapelle.

Susan Knutsen for her photographs covering the 'Golden Hind'.

Ms Ramone Kilpatrick of the Copyright Licensing Agency Ltd., including the Authors Licensing and Copyright Society and the Design and Artistic Copyright Society with reference to Stuart E Beck's Ships, Boats and Craft.

Ms Margaret Ferre of HMSO Norwich with reference to 'Ship Models From Earliest Times to 1700'.

Much of the information and historical references used show varying opinions, in these instances the majority views have been taken to describe the various vessels featured.

FOREWORD

Old sailing ships, like old houses, underwent many alterations in their lifetime. Hulls of one type may be fitted out in the fashion of another type so true identification can sometimes be difficult. What work they had to do and the waters they had to sail on dictated their rig, fittings and hull shapes. Collier barques or brigs, strongly built for coal carrying, have ended up as refitted exploration vessels like Captain Cook's 'Endeavour'. Sprit rigged barges were given new masts and turned into ketch rigged barges for coastal trading.

Many sails were of mixed variety. Trial and error, with little scientific knowledge seems to have accounted for the many sail plans tried.

Because some merchant types were converted to auxiliary war vessels in times of trouble, extra timbers were installed to support the ordnance carried and because of this there is no separate war vessel section but mention has been made in the text when certain types were used as warships, irrespective of original classification.

Around the coast of the British Isles there were scores of smallish fishing and other vessels working from harbours, estuaries and beaches.

Some of the local names of these vessels are listed below, their names give little indication of their type but the locals knew what they meant.

Baldie	Nabby
Mumble-bee	Nobby
Boggy	Picarooner
Cauf	Pram
Doble	Shoe
Flash boat	Shout
Folyer	Shinerman
Funny	Stumpy
Gabbart	Stacky
Lerret	Tosher
Mulie	Zulu

Some you will find in this book.

INTRODUCTION

Historical ship enthusiasts will always take the opportunity to discuss and argue about their interest in watercraft of all ages. Historians, artists, model makers, sailors or those of us who just like ships and boats can spend hours discussing the subject.

It is an ancient and detailed story full of adventure. Floating vessels were one of man's first types of major transportation and have continued to develop over thousands of years. The availability of suitable building materials and individual needs and local conditions to a large extent directed the final size and shapes of these vessels and the progress they made.

The early boat builders who lived in or near wooded areas were very lucky. Other less fortunate builders developed ingenious methods using little wood but other materials such as animal skins, whale and other animal bone, wickerwork and reeds, the unique qualities of the materials shaping the development of many early and distinctive vessels.

As water mobility increased so did the exchange of ideas; this cross-fertilisation produced many types of new craft. Not all of these types have been featured here but most of the important ones have. The following illustrations and descriptive details may help enthusiasts name the type and rough date of individual craft throughout the subject's long and varied history from early BC to the turn of the 19th century, or thereabouts.

The four sections of the book have been loosely divided into

Ancient craft

Sailing ships

Small sailing ships, boats and craft

Steam ships and boats

The last section includes both screw and paddle-driven vessels built up to 1900 or just beyond.

It is not the intention to show every craft but a good number in an easy-to-use reference book. Some vessels found in the small sailing ship section might qualify to be in the larger vessel section as sizes varied considerably within the same type and class of vessels. The general classification regarding size is loosely followed. A few vessels illustrated were not strictly 19th century but are included as boats of interest. I hope this explanation will appease the purist.

ANCIENT CRAFT

FLEMISH CARRACK CIRCA 1480

This large trading vessel of both northern and southern Europe developed from the 14th to the 17th centuries. A complete change from single-masted vessels to three-masted vessels took place during the 15th century. The square rig on fore and main-masts with lateen rig on the mizzen formed the basic arrangement of rigging. Another important difference for naval architecture was the introduction of carvel building of the hull. This new system provided much stronger hulls for the increasing weights of ordnance carried. High two-decked forecastles were typical of the carrack with round sterns surmounted with a slightly lower stern castle. The illustration shows a Flemish Carrack of 1480. No main top masts nor sprit-sails had come into use, the mizzen sail being used as a steering sail. Heavy timber wales were fitted with vertical fenders crossing these amidships. These vessels were universally used for war and for trading.

THE CATALAN BOAT CIRCA 1440

This strange looking boat is drawn from a model. The original model now resides in the Prins Hendrick Museum in Rotterdam. It is probably the earliest original European model of a sailing ship. In the early part of the 20th century the original model hung in the Hermitage of San Simon de Mataro, Spain. It disappeared from where it had hung for many years, turning up eventually in a Munich flea market in 1920. A Mr. Van Beuningen, a wealthy Dutchman, acquired it and presented it to the Museum in Rotterdam where it is now considered to be a model of great significance, giving rise to many theories concerning vessels of around the 1440s.

SHIP OF THE CINQUE PORTS 13TH CENTURY

Ship designs were beginning to change in the 13th century. Broader hulls with depth were built to carry the large type of square sail. The images of these vessels came from contemporary seals of the ancient towns of the south coast of England. The Dover seal was used in preparing a model from which this illustration was made. It is estimated that hulls of this period had considerable sheer and were clincher-built with an approximate length of 75-80ft. and a 25ft. beam. The steer-board is like those of Viking ships but in the Dover seal is shown on the port side.

EGYPTIAN SHIP CIRCA 1300BC

Good hard and softwood trees have always been scarce in Egypt. The acacia tree pro-vided rather short irregular timbers to build serviceable vessels. Cedar was eventually imported from the Lebanon for some of the more vital parts. The spoon-shaped hulls were built without stem or sternpost timbers, keel or ribs. Planking was joined together with various dowels, cordage, pegs and wedges. The heavy deck beams made up for the absence of a rib construction. To keep this kind of craft rigid, a very strong truss rope was fitted from stem to stern. There were many different types and sizes of these rather unattractive craft. A small version is illustrated.

FLEMISH CARRACK
CIRCA 1480

THE CATALAN BOAT
CIRCA 1440

SHIP OF THE
CINQUE PORTS
13TH CENTURY

EGYPTIAN SHIP
CIRCA 1300BC

ENGLISH SHIP 1426

The details of this early vessel were taken from the seal of John, Duke of Bedford. It relates to the office of Lord High Admiral of England and shows a fine example of a 15th century vessel. A clincher-built ship of about 60ft in length, it had a median rudder mounted on a sternpost instead of a steerboard. To accommodate a vertical rudder, a certain amount of deadwood was needed in the keel. This new shape of hull gave a distinct difference between bow and stern. The forecastle was the fighting platform, the after-castle or summer-castle was extended to provide cabin accommodation for important passengers.

ENGLISH SHIP 1485

A large ship or 'cog', details of which are held in the British Museum. It is fairly certain that this is what an English ship of this period looked like. Clincher-built and with bluff bow and stern this double-ended ship had a straight sternpost providing a good support for a sturdy rudder. A summer-castle covered the poop area and forward a triangular forecastle jutted out over the high prow.

The rigging consisted of a foremast with square sail. A large square sail on the main mast with a lateen sail on the mizzen.

ASSYRIAN GALLEY 700 BC

Assyria, a kingdom of Mesopotamia, stretched along the banks of the Euphrates and Tigris rivers. This early civilisation evolved over 4000 years and by 700 BC had developed large galley ram ships. The illustration shows an impression of one of these ships, the details of which come from ancient stone monuments of Assyrian origin. The people of this kingdom were commercial and warlike - material gain and their own supremacy was of prime importance giving impetus to the construction of ships for trade and war - like this vessel of King Sennachirib's navy (705-681 BC).

GREEK GALLEY CIRCA 500 BC

A Greek trireme had an extremely long hull in relation to the beam, with a length of about 150ft.. and breadth of 16ft., over the outriggers 19ft. Because of the need for longitudinal strength, heavy timber wales extended from end to end with the lower wale connecting with the forward-projecting keel forming an efficient ram at water level. There are many theories about the position and numbers of oarsmen that sat in two or three tiers on each side. At the top there were 31 oars with the middle and lower banks containing 27 oars a side - 170 in all. These triremes dominated the Mediterranean area 2,500 years ago.

PHOENICIAN TRADING SHIP 600BC

Phoenicia was situated in an area of north west Syria, stretching down to the Lebanon. Phoenician colonies were also to be found in many coastal areas of the Mediterranean. These ancient traders and craftsmen travelled to many areas in Europe; their artefacts have been found in archaeological sites throughout the area. They were fine navigators and understood ways of using the sun and the Pole Star to plot their long journeys far

ENGLISH SHIP
1426

ENGLISH SHIP
1485

ASSYRIAN GALLEY
700 BC

GREEK GALLEY
CIRCA 500 BC

beyond the normal limits of the period. Herodotus, 484-425 BC described their journeys around Africa.

Cedarwood grew well in the Lebanon and was used extensively in their shipbuilding; some of this timber found its way into Egypt for a similar purpose. The illustration shows a trading vessel of 600 BC Like all ships of this period a large square sail supported on a central mast with yards was the favoured rig that drove these ancient travellers slowly but surely (with oars on occasions when the winds failed).

ROMAN MERCHANT SHIP 2ND CENTURY AD

As Mediterranean commerce, particularly in corn, increased so the development of a broad beamed type of merchant ship was introduced, discarding oars and relying on sail power only. The illustration is drawn from a model, the detail of which came from contemporary reliefs and other images. This type of vessel would have sailed between Rome and the coasts of Egypt including the Levant. Their capacity was about 250 tons, the size of the hull some 90ft. long overall. These ships had a definite stem and a less pronounced sternpost, a strong keel and two or more heavy wales. Some sail plans show a square topsail in addition to main sail.

'SANTA MARIA' 1492 (GALICIAN NAO)

The largest of the three ships in the small fleet of Columbus that set sail for what was called his "Enterprise of the Indies" on 3rd August 1492. As the flagship, the 'Santa Maria' was a Galician Nao (ship), the other two, namely the 'Nina' and the 'Pinta', were caravels. Nobody can say for certain what the flagship looked like for Columbus returned to Europe in the 'Nina' leaving his ship in the Americas. Some years ago a full-size reconstruction in the harbour in Barcelona was moored. Sizes of these vessels are only approximate. The 'Santa Maria' 95ft. long, the 'Nina' and the 'Pinta' 56ft. and 58ft. overall. The rig of the 'Santa Maria' had three masts; the mizzen carried a lateen sail, the mainmast two square sails, a course and topsail, the foremast a single square sail.

Two caravels, a relatively small Mediterranean trading vessel. The 'Nina' was rigged as a conventional ship, like the 'Santa Maria' and the 'Pinta lateen-rigged.

VIKING SHIP

Viking Drakkars (dragon ships) are one of the first ancient vessels that we have positive knowledge of. In Scandinavia there are well-preserved hulls in museums that have survived burial for many hundreds of years. The majority were-not large vessels; sizes ranged between 10 and 25 metres long with 24 oarsmen or more. One larger vessel described in old Norse tales was 120ft. long carrying 64 oarsmen. Clinker-planked with rib construction was typical of all Nordic ships, giving the hull a certain flexibility. Many long voyages were made from the Viking settlements in Southern Scandinavia. Armies landed in England at various times from 787 to 825. Hamburg was plundered in 836, Iceland was settled in 861 and Vikings reached Greenland in 983 and America in 1000 AD. All the journeys were made in these open craft driven by one large square sail and rowing oarsmen.

PHOENICIAN TRADING SHIP
600BC

ROMAN MERCHANT SHIP
2ND CENTURY AD

'SANTA MARIA' 1492
(GALICIAN NAO)

VIKING SHIP

SAILING SHIPS

BARQUE 1770

Barque, or bark was a three-masted vessel with square sails on all masts. The mizzen carried a lower fore-and-aft sail as in the illustration. These vessels were medium size sailing ships up to the mid 19th century but were later built much larger with four masts and, later still, five masts: the usual square rig on four masts and fore-and-aft sails on the fifth mast with between-mast staysails.

The original barques were used for the transportation of goods and as traders. Collier barques were built at Whitby; Captain Cook used one of these in 1768 when he made his famous voyages of exploration in HMS 'Endeavour', as illustrated. The ship had a major refit before this famous voyage.

FOUR-MASTED BARQUE

Until the mid 19th century three-masted barques were relatively small sailing ships, but later in the century and into the 20th century this type of vessel was made larger, up to 3,000 tons. These ships were involved with grain and nitrate trades. Four - and even five-masted barques were later built, ranging up to roughly 5,000 tons. Another ship in the same family and period was the Jackass Barque, a four-masted vessel, square-rigged on the foremast and second mast, fore-and-aft rigged on the third and fourth masts. The skippers of these ships involved in the nitrate trade considered this mixed rig more efficient and safer in stormy weather around Cape Horn when sailing to Chile.

BARQUENTINE 1820

The barquentine rig developed around the 1800s, with three masts and a hull about the size of a barque. This new rig consisted of a full set of square sails set on the foremast and fore-and-aft sails set on the main and mizzenmasts carrying gaffs with topsails. There were slight variations like two square sails only and one gaff sail on the foremast and mainmast. These were sometimes called topsail schooners to classify this hybrid. In Sicilian waters barquetines were square-rigged on the foremast and carried lateen sails on the main and mizzen. All these rig changes were an effort to reduce crew sizes, necessary with square sails on all masts.

'TERRE NEUVA' BARQUENTINE

Not only American and Canadian vessels fished the Grand Banks. In St. Malo and from Fecamp in France sturdy schooner barque or barquentine ships would cross the Atlantic to fish for cod and other fish. Like the American schooners these French vessels carried a dozen or more rowing dories on deck for line fishing. Some of these ships were about 1000 tons, carrying 50 crewmen.

BARQUE 1770

FOUR-MASTED
BARQUE

BARQUENTINE
1820

'TERRE NEUVA'
BARQUENTINE

BILANDER

From the Dutch bijlander, a small European merchant ship of the 17th and 18th centuries. The foremast of this two-masted vessel carried a course and square topsail, the mainmast was rigged with a four-cornered lateen rig, or what was known as bilander-rigged with square topsails. These vessels were similar to a brig but the hull was almost flat-bottomed. Bilanders could be seen as far apart as the North Sea and the Mediterranean and were widely built in Holland, Sweden and England. Their main purpose was to carry goods into shallow waters of coastal areas and inland water routes. At the end of the 19th century freight barges were referred to as bilanders. The original bilanders were made up to 100 tons.

BRITISH NAVAL BRIG

The term brig was an abbreviation of brigantine but later a brig became a ship in her own right, square-rigged on both masts. Brigs were used for short coastal trading voyages. In the British Navy they were widely used also by European navies as training ships but there have been many that were used in wartime with a single deck that could carry 18 guns. One famous man-of-war brig, built in England at the beginning of the 19th century called HMS 'Grasshopper', found fame in the Dutch Navy after being captured in 1811 and renamed 'Irene'.

COLLIER BRIG & SCHOONERS

Sailing colliers were used extensively in the 17th, 18th and 19th centuries. Although there were purpose-built collier brigs like the Northumbrian 'cat-built' vessels, many types were involved in coal carrying like the schooner and other three-masted vessels. Sea coal from the northeastern coast of Britain was carried to London and other destinations. A feature of a typical collier was its straight stem without figurehead and exceptionally large jib sail. An approximate dimension was 100ft. by 25ft. Ships could carry 200 to 300 tons of coal.

In some coastal areas where beaches were suitable and not shelved, brigs and schooners could beach on an ebbing tide and be unloaded using horses and carts over the sand. In London and other large ports, vessels would unload into river lighters moored alongside by a system known as 'coal-whipping'. By modern standards the amount of coal carried by these vessels was small but in sufficient quantities for domestic use in Britain.

BRIGANTINE & BRIG-SCHOONER

The term brigantine was originally the name describing a 16th century type of oared and sailing warship in the Mediterranean used by brigand pirates. This illustration shows a 19th century brigantine, known also as a brig-schooner.

A two masted vessel setting square sails on the foremast and fore-and-aft sails on the mainmast. Some Northern European brigantines had square topsails on the second upper mast as well as carrying fore-and-aft sails on the lower mast known as a Hermaphrodite Brig. The Brigantine was a fast trading ship of medium size. Some were used in the triangular trade routes across the Atlantic and some versions could also be found operating in the Black Sea during the mid 1800s.

BILANDER

BRITISH
NAVAL BRIG

COLLIER BRIG
& SCHOONERS

BRIGANTINE &
BRIG-SCHOONER

MODERN BRIGANTINE

This has been included to illustrate a modern-built brigantine - a rare vessel nowadays. Colin Mudie, a Scottish-born naval architect, designed this modern version that was presented by Britain to mark the Australian Bicentenary in 1988. The British-Australian Trust referred to it as a 35 metre schooner but the vessel is technically a brigantine made of steel.

HERRING BUSS

Throughout three centuries until about the early 1700s, net fishing in the North Sea was carried out by these heavy square-rigged drifters known as busses, a term thought to be old French - busse - meaning cask, perhaps denoting barrel shape; other theories prevail though. Handier types of rig developed after the 18th century like the lugger and ketch rig for fishing.

The medium sized buss illustrated would have been around 58ft. long by 15ft. beam of 56 tons burden. The 16th century herring buss had three masts, sometimes two, each carrying one square sail. The mainmast had an additional topsail hoisted on a topmast, scarfed into the lower mast. Both foremast and mainmast could be lowered to rest on a stout gallow support at the break of the poop deck when drifting nets; there were no foredecks as such. Merchant ship busses were also used throughout Europe and the Mediterranean for trading purposes.

GENOESE CARRACK 16TH CENTURY

A three-masted merchant vessel of the 15th and 16th centuries, heavily built, beamy and bluff-bowed with a narrower swept up stern. These ships were clumsy sailors but with their lateen mizzens, a great improvement on earlier ships.

The illustration shows this Genoese vessel armed. Other countries also used carracks of slightly different designs.

CARAVEL 1500

The caravel was a medium to small trading vessel of Mediterranean design, active over a long period starting in the 14th century and still in use in the 17th century. There were many versions with differing hull designs used by the French, Spanish, Portuguese and Swedish merchants and navies.

The Spanish and Portuguese started using caravels for their many voyages of exploration and trade in the 15th century. A large version is illustrated. The caravel was originally lateen-rigged on two or three masts and square-rigged on the foremast. Later three masts were adopted with the fore and main square-rigged and with mizzen lateen-rigged. This sailplan was used especially on long sea or ocean journeys. The average length of a three-masted caravel was 75-80ft. The 'Santa Maria', flagship of Columbus, was 95ft. long. The other two ships of his small squadron in 1492, the 'Pinta', 58ft. and the 'Nina', 56ft. were all caravels with slightly differing hull lines and sail plans. Various terms were used to denote sail plans: namely, caravela latina and caravela rotunda.

C.O.I.

MODERN BRIGANTINE

HERRING BUSS

GENOESE CARRACK
16TH CENTURY

CARAVEL
1500

PORTUGUSE CARAVELA 1535

In the Mediterranean of the 16th century there were many types of sailing ship originating from the galley, for instance the galeasse, an oared galleon, the carrack and the caravela, a vessel with a hull similar to a galleon but with bows having an extended beak without a figure head, suggestive of the galley. The ship illustrated is based on one of the caravelas used by Emperor Charles V at the capture of Tunis in 1535. Other information on this ship comes from contemporary tapestries preserved in Madrid. The vessel was approximately 114ft. long with a 30ft. beam of 400 tons burden lateen-rigged on three masts and square-rigged on the foremast. At this period south European vessels were gradually replacing the lateen rig with square sails.

PORTUGUSE
CARAVELA 1535

SAILING CLIPPERS 1868

Foreign competition, almost entirely from America, gave British ship builders and ship owners a spur to develop faster trading ships in the mid 19th century with much improved sailing qualities. English, and particularly Scottish yards, began building clipper ships for the tea and other trading in the 1860s. Famous named ships took part in clipper runs from ports in China like Foochow in 1866. 'Fiery Cross', 'Ariel', 'Taeping', 'Serica' and the 'Taitsing' all reached London within two days of one another on one such race. In 1872 the 'Thermopylae' illustrated here raced the 'Cutty Sark' from Foochow. The opening of the Suez Canal in 1869 began a decline in this type of ship and although they switched to carrying wool from Australia they were soon outmoded in a trade in which large cargoes, small crews and less speed were more economical. Large four and five-masted steel barques provided this type of cargo transport until steam arrived as a new power source for trading ships.

Lloyds' Register shows that in 1910-11 there were only 957 sailing vessels over 100 tons burden owned by firms in the UK. As steam took over from sail, companies owning large sailing vessels made great efforts to reduce the number of crews needed for sail management. Many labour-saving devices were introduced like donkey engines to trim the yards and hoist sails, double topsails and topgallants. These various labour-saving devices were not introduced to improve the sailor's lot but the owners' declining profits. A 2,000 ton vessel could now manage with 18 able seamen whereas an old 1,000 ton tea clipper could need 35 to 40 men. 'Thermopylae' had a 212ft. hull with 36ft. beam, she was one of the largest clippers, weighing nearly 1,000 tons.

COPER 1880

A heavy bluff-bowed trader of Dutch origin that became a kind of floating supply vessel to the many fishermen working the Dogger Bank and North Sea fishing areas in the mid to late 19th century. The catches could be exchanged for essential supplies when fishermen were forced to lie idle at sea through calms or lack of shoal fishing. Inevitably these floating shops became floating grog shops, supplying cheap spirits to the fishermen. By 1890 these vessels were abolished.

CORVETTE 1800

The corvette was a lightly-armed war vessel with a flush deck carrying a single tier of about 20 guns, similar to a frigate but smaller and ship-rigged on three masts. The design was originally French, a development of the lateen-rigged galley with virtually the same hull form being used in the corvette. The fast, useful ship was adopted by the British Navy: the best ones built of cedarwood in Bermuda. The flush deck construction was particularly suitable for service in hot climates, the open deck admitted free circulation of air. These vessels carried oars or long sweeps for quick manoeuvring in light airs. The oars were worked through small opening oar ports, beside the gun ports.

SAILING CLIPPER
1868

COPER
1880

CORVETTE
1800

DUTCH FLEUTE

Fleute or vliete as a term to describe this vessel first appeared at the end of the 16th century. The word meant 'to flow', no doubt referring to what was considered harmonious lines in these famous Dutch cargo vessels. Their capacity for cargo was considerably higher than that of other ships of the period. Originally the foremast and mainmast carried two square sails each with a lateen sail on the mizzen as in this illustration. Larger versions with longer masts rigged a third square topsail on the first and second masts; the mizzen carried a square topsail above the lateen sail. The bowsprit supported an additional mast to which a small square sail was rigged above the lower bow spritsail, which was also square. The very narrow, swept-up stern featured an oval opening for the tiller. The decks were narrower than other types of the period due to the acute tumblehome of the fulsome hull. The fleute was considered one of the ships that made Holland rich as a maritime nation. The long rounded stern with its opening was originally designed to bring huge pine trees from Scandinavia to be used as masts and other timbers for shipbuilding.

BRITISH NAVAL FRIGATE 1840

Frigates were a class of ship to be found in the navies of most seafaring nations. Rated in the British Navy as 5th or 6th raters they were not expected to lie in the first line of battle. Armaments consisted of between 24 and 38 guns carried on a single open gun deck. Their sailing qualities were considered better than the larger rated ships of the Navy so they were used as look-outs for the main first line ships, passing on Admiralty signals to the fleet. They could work independently of the main fleet, cruising in search of privateers or as escort ships for merchant convoys. The first frigates, as a class, appeared about the 1640s. The illustration shows a ship of the 1840s when they reached their prime efficiency. Average length 100ft., 26ft. beam. It was fully square-rigged on three masts and with a crew of approximately 130 men.

VENETIAN GALEASSE

This vessel is a compromise between the oared galley and the galleon. Oars were retained in the galeasse to provide driving power whatever the wind condition. Because of the need to accommodate oarsmen, cannons and huge lateen sails, the vessels were built with a greater beam than the galleons. Two or three masts set vertical with varying sizes of forecastles and stern structuring, they were not as manoeuvrable as the galley, suffering inevitable defects because of compromise between the two types of craft.

One famous sea battle where galleys and galeasses took part was in 1571 in Greek waters around the area of the Gulf of Lepanto, between the Christians and the Turks. The Christians won due to the power of the Venetian galeasses, the wider decks and higher sides allowing more firepower to be directed on the enemy.

DUTCH FLEUTE

BRITISH NAVAL
FRIGATE 1840

VENETIAN GALEASSE

ELIZABETHAN GALLEON 16TH CENTURY

The upper stern structure of Elizabethan ships was not as high and ungainly as that of early Tudor vessels. The round stern had been replaced by a square tuck or transom stern. Later in the century ships were fitted with projecting galleries extending along each quarter and across the stern. Elaborate figureheads and stern decoration of the Royal Arms formed the main embellishment. Whip-staff steering connected to the fore end of the tiller below deck gave a rather inefficient method of steering. Long projecting beakheads followed the line of the wales decorated in contrasting colours.

The main armament of large galleons consisted of brass and cast iron muzzleloaders: culverin and demi-culverin, demi-cannon and cannon perier and other types firing shot of many sizes from 32 and 24lb to 3 and 4lb cannon balls.

Throughout Elizabeth's reign four masts including the 'Bonaventure' rear mizzen masts were on most vessels and in James Is navy this continued until half the King's ships had four masts. Foremast and main were square-rigged, the third and mizzen were lateen-rigged. By 1618 all English men-of-war were fitted with square mizzen topsails. The additional power obtained by this and the lengthening of the mizzen meant the fourth mast was unnecessary.

By the end of the 16th century the high forecastles were reduced giving better manoeuvrability. Later, in Spain, this idea was incorporated into Spanish warship galleons and in trading ships replacing the carrack.

GALLIOT 1850

The name originally meant a small galley sailed and rowed by 16 or 20 oars, with a single mast. During the 18th century it became the accepted term to describe a Dutch trading vessel with a barge-like hull, leeboards and fore-and-aft rigged. Although the illustration shows a two-masted vessel the early craft had only one mast, sometimes sprit-rigged. In the mid 1800s the galliot was one of the most widely built ships in north Germany and was used extensively in the North Sea. These cargo vessels not only plied the northern coastal waters but also made journeys to America and the Cape. Seal hunters and whalers used galliots and the French developed mortar vessels known as 'galiotes á bombes'.

'GOLDEN HIND'

This is the ship in which Francis Drake circumnavigated the world from 1577 to 1580. Originally named the 'Pelican', Drake changed the name to 'Golden Hind' when he reached the Magellan Straits in honour of his patron Sir Christopher Hatton whose family crest was a hind (see stern picture). She was the only ship of the five vessels that set sail to make the journey back to Plymouth reaching there on 26th September 1580. The photo illustrations are of the modern replica of this small galleon. The sails were square-rigged on the foremast and main, lateen-rigged on the mizzen, spritsail on the bowsprit. Length 50ft. x 19ft. beam, weight 190 tons burden.

When the ship was built, possibly at Deptford, East London, she was a small galleon very well-built with a double-sheathed hull. She was well-equipped and carried ample ordnance and crew of about 90 men.

ELIZABETHAN GALLEON
16TH CENTURY

GALLIOT 1850

'GOLDEN HIND'

HOY

The hoy had no definite characteristics as such, being a small to medium coasting vessel up to 60 tons working in British and Continental waters during the 16th to 19th centuries. It had a single mast carrying a loose-footed mainsail, square topsail, foresail and jib. Some Dutch versions had two masts and leeboards with tonnage up to 40 tons; some of these were lug-rigged. Their uses were varied and included carrying passengers from port to port in which case cabins were erected, re-supplying warships at sea and loading or off-loading larger cargo vessels. An average size was 80ft. long, 21ft. beam with a 12ft. depth of hold.

HULK

The word hulk goes back a long way. It generally describes any large unwieldy ship of simple construction with rounded bow and stern, not unlike a carrack. In the early 18th and 19th centuries old ships, no longer safe to make ocean journeys, were moored in harbours and were used in a number of different ways. Demasted and roofed they served as floating warehouses and storage vessels, as temporary billets for soldiers and naval personnel, as quarantine ships and were sometimes fitted out for use in stepping or lifting masts out of sea-going ships in harbour. They were notoriously used as prison ships, giving the inmates a severe mode of punishment. Thames hulks were introduced in 1776 to contain the overflowing prison population of that period.

BALTIC KETCH

A trading vessel built of wood and used extensively in northern waters in the latter part of the 19th and 20th centuries. Although known as a ketch, yards are crossed on the main mast and the topsail is a very square fore-and-aft sail, similar to a Tasmanian ketch. A built up surface cabin is set below or integrated with mizzenmast base.

FRENCH KETCH 1750

There were various types of ketches developed during the mid 1700s. A two-masted vessel rigged usually with square sails on the mainmast and fore-and-aft sails on the mizzenmast stepped before the rudder. It was used mostly for fishing and cargo work in coastal areas but could be armed in war when needed. The original name in England was 'catch'. This suggests they were used for fishing but their primary use was as a coasting trade vessel.

Very early ketches were smallish vessels around 50 tons or less. The name ketch refers to the sail rig more than the vessel as a type. In the wars of the 17th and 18th centuries, French, English and Dutch ketches were built in great numbers as tenders to the fleets. The English adapted them as floating platforms for their heavy mortars, building in strong deck and beam timbers to take this heavy ordnance positioned forward of the main mast. Some three-masted hulls had their foremasts removed to facilitate these large mortars.

The ketches of mid 19th century were two-masted, fore-and-aft vessels illustrated elsewhere.

HOY

HULK

BALTIC KETCH

FRENCH KETCH 1750

TASMANIAN KETCH

The distinctive topsails of this ketch look like modified lugsails. They are unusual in having a light boom laced to the foot of the sail, not unlike the Baltic ketch. The sizes of these ketches ranged from 10 to 90 tons. In Hobart and Launceston where these boats were usually built they carried out many tasks. Store carrying to the outlying coastal districts returning with farm produce and timber was one of the main uses.

DUTCH KLIPPER

A sailing cargo vessel usually built of steel and generally ketch-rigged carrying leeboards. Her cargo capacity was similar to a barge and working areas were also similar. The mast was in a tabernacle to facilitate lowering, often needed when working the inland waterways. The vessel carried a huge horizontal steering wheel, useful in narrow rivers.

LIGHTSHIPS

Normally a lightship is dumb; it has no engine and is towed out and positioned by a tug or lighthouse tender. Dangerous navigation areas around our coasts and the entrances to large estuaries are the usual places where these vessels are positioned. The illustration shows an early lightship in which the central mast passes through the lamp, which could be lowered to the deck for attention. During the daytime, 'day marks' could be hoisted: these were different shapes to distinguish the various lightships. Most ships were painted red and were named. The positions of these vessels were always noted on navigation charts, as they are today. Lanby buoys today are replacing many lightships. These automatic navigation aids are unmanned but provide the same service as the old lightships. The average length of the old type ships was 100ft. by 20ft. beam.

ARMED LUGGER

Smuggling and privateering ventures were well served both in England and France, by this type of three-masted vessel in the late 1700s and early 1800s. The British navy also took some into service. The armed lugger is said to have evolved from the Chasse-Maree, a French coastal fishing vessel during the Revolutionary and Napoleonic periods. The old original lugger rigs were refined and tuned to provide a more efficient and fast sailing ship.

Masts were raked aft and the mizzen stepped tight up on the ship's transom. A long bowsprit fitted with bumpkin chain enabled a large spread of canvas to be rigged. A large crew was carried due to the need for providing gun crews and sail management both at the same time on many occasions. The average length of the vessel was 60 to 70ft.

'MAYFLOWER'

This historic vessel carried the Pilgrim Fathers from Plymouth to New England in 1620. The small merchant ship was not a new vessel and records show she was about 180 tons burden. Her journey to America started from Southampton together with the companion ship 'Speedwell', but the 'Speedwell' was found to be unseaworthy and both ships put in at Plymouth. The 'Mayflower' sailed alone from Plymouth on the

TASMANIAN KETCH

DUTCH KLIPPER

LIGHTSHIPS

ARMED LUGGER

6th September 1620 carrying 100 passengers. They reached Provincetown Harbour on 11th November 1620. Their final landing was at a place that is now Plymouth, Massachusetts, on 21st December. Historians can only imagine what this small ship looked like exactly and are guided by other ships of this type and period.

'MAYFLOWER'

NEW YORK PILOT BOAT

Purpose-built pilot boats were being used before the American Revolution. The original vessels of this type are said to have originated in the Chesapeake area but by 1812 various important coastal ports had developed their own particular versions of these fast weatherly craft. New York, Boston, New Jersey and Virginia feature in their development. Local requirements dictated by weather and local sea conditions had much to do with the final design and sail plan. Although most were two-masted, fore-and-aft schooner rigged craft, the Sandy Hook pilot schooner could raise square sails on the mainmast as well as fore-and-aft canvas. Keen competition flourished as trade along the east coast increased which drove vessels further out to sea whilst plying and searching for business. Under these conditions hulls were designed to be deeper; sizes varied. The large pilots were 100ft. with 23ft. beam, smaller vessels were under 80ft. overall.

NEW YORK PILOT BOAT
1800

BOSTON PILOT BOAT
1884

VIRGINIAN PILOT BOAT
1806

POLACRE

A Mediterranean sailing ship used in the 16th and 17th centuries. A distinguishing feature of this Italian vessel was its pole mast (no topmast section): this was square-rigged with lateen sails on the foremast. The slow transition in the Mediterranean from lateen to square sails resulted in various rigs as the illustration here shows. The pole mast was preferred as it enabled yards to be lowered when required like the lateen rig masts. The French used these ships as trading vessels but guns would be carried in times of war or when trading near Africa's northern coasts where corsair pirates preyed on merchant vessels.

HMS PRINCE 1670

HMS 'Prince' is a good example of a capital warship of the mid 17th century. The details that we know come from contemporary dockyard-built models, which are very accurate. The 'Prince' carried a crew of 780 men, her keel length measured 131ft. beam 45ft.8ins., depth of hold 19ft. She was heavily armed with 100 guns ranging from 42 pounders to 3 pounders on her lower gun-decks, quarterdeck and forecastle. Unlike continental ships with transom sterns, the English ships of this period were being built with a round tuck stern where the planking is curved and carries into a rabbet joint at the sternpost. In 1692 the 'Prince' was broken up when some of her timbers went into building the 'Royal William'.

FIRST RATER 1805

The word rate was used from 1751 to identify and grade the six divisions into which warships of sailing navies were listed. The number of guns carried gave the ships their rate. Ships of 100 to 110 guns were 1st raters, as in this illustration; 2nd raters carried 84, later 90 to 100 guns; 3rd raters carried 70 to 84 guns; 4th raters 50 to 70; 5th raters 32 to 50 and 6th raters any number of guns up to 32 if commanded by a post-captain. When commanded by a commander these were rated as sloops of war. HMS 'Victory' in a permanent dock at Portsmouth, England, is a fine example of a first rater of the late 1700s.

FIRST RATER
1805

POLACRE

HMS PRINCE
1670

THIRD RATER 1812

Of the six classifications of 18th and 19th century warships, first, second and third raters were the ships considered sufficiently powerful to be in the direct line of battle in action with opposing fleets. The third rater illustrated would have carried between 70 and 84 guns on two main gun decks, top deck and poop. An average size of a 3rd rater was approximately 170 to 180ft. long with a 45ft. beam.

GLOUCESTER SCHOONER 1900

The Gloucester fishing schooner developed fine lines during a twenty-year period from about 1880. Captain Joseph William Collins published papers advocating major improvements for the offshore cod fishing fleets of the American east coast. This culminated in the building of 'Grampus' for the United States Fish Commission. Many famous schooners followed, the 'Helen B. Thomas', 'Rose Dorothea', built by Sir Thomas Lipton, the 'James W. Parker', the 'Harry Belden' and many others.

The foretopmast and foremast were both made shorter on these new schooners and the new wire rigging replaced the old hemp ropes that had been used for centuries. Deep sloping keels and heavy ballasting enabled these fishing schooners to make very fast passages from fishing grounds, sailing close to the wind back to the various fish marketing ports of the American seaboard. They carried various numbers of dories stowed each side on deck amidships. These were used for line fishing when on the fishing grounds.

GREAT LAKES SCHOONER

These three-masted schooners were employed in the lumber, grain, ore and coal trades on the five Great Lakes of Canada and the USA. The size of individual schooners varied according to the service they served. Some were two-masted, others four-masted. One interesting feature of some types was the triangular 'raffee' topsail on the foremast. Some of the smaller class was fitted with centre-plates. The illustration shows a schooner of about 260 tons.

GREAT LAKES SCHOONER

THIRD RATER
1812

GLOUCESTER
SCHOONER 1900

39

TERN SCHOONER 1875

American schooner builders had been developing the three-masted, fore-and-aft rigs since around the 1800s. Speed was an important factor during the wars of the early 19th century. It was a successful sailing ship but as the size increased so did the problems of sail handling in early versions. Sizes ranged between 75 and 150 ft. in length of hull. An example of an 1875 vessel was approximately 105ft. long with a 25ft. beam and a 10ft. hold. Many two-masted versions, like the Gloucester schooner, were used in the fishing trade. The Great Lake schooners with three masts were employed in the lumber, grain, ore and coal trades. The name 'Tern' means 'a series of three' and in Nova Scotia this name was used widely to describe a three-master with fore-and-aft rig.

TOPSAIL SCHOONER

The topsail schooner was in its time a very popular vessel used in the British coasting trade. Although the two masts carried fore-and-aft sails, the original types carried yards crossed on the foremast to rig one, sometimes two square sails. With the advance in rig designs, these were changed to jib headed or jackyard-topsails. Small schooner yachts today normally set Bermuda sails thus not needing topsails.

SCOW 1900

Scows were of many sizes from about 25 to 200 tons and still exist today; a craft full in the bilges and with a flatish bottom used as lighters or as ferry craft. There are many types - in North America they are broad in the beam and flat-bottomed with bilge keels. The illustration shows a New Zealand scow employed in the carriage of timber, coal, grain and other heavy cargoes. The hulls were usually built of wood, an average size 80 tons and would carry a crew of six. A broad square stern is a feature of these craft; they were usually schooner rigged.

SNOW

A two-masted merchant vessel spanning many years of use from 16th to 19th century. These vessels were entirely a European ship, rigged as a brig with square sails on both masts. Snows were the largest two-masted vessels of their period with tonnage of up to 1,000. One distinguishing feature was the small trysail mast stepped immediately abaft the mainmast from which a trysail with boom was set. The luff of this sail was hooped to the extra mast. Some vessels replaced the trysail mast in favour of a horse on the mainmast to which the luff of the trysail was attached by rings.

SNOW

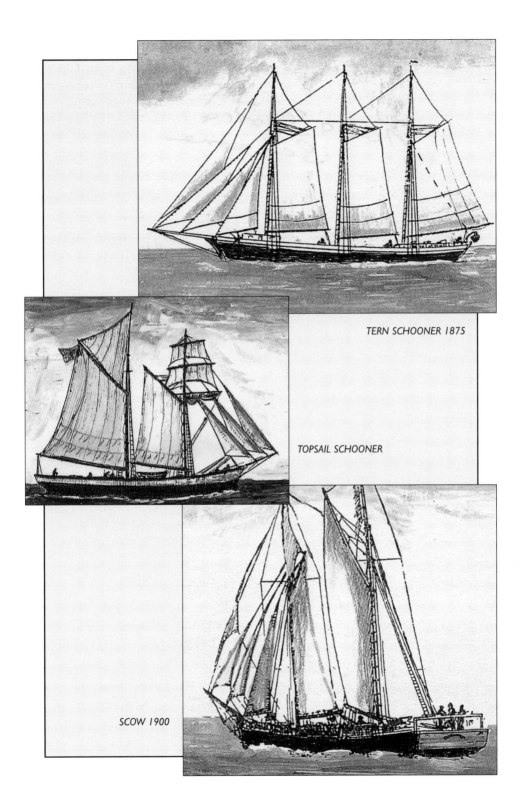

TERN SCHOONER 1875

TOPSAIL SCHOONER

SCOW 1900

41

CONCARNEAU TUNNY BOAT

A yawl-rigged fishing boat of around 50 to 60 tons, used for deep-sea tunny fishing. Long rods rigged on each side of the vessel trail several lines. These strong sea boats stayed fishing usually for two weeks then returned to port. Rods were stowed against the mast when not in use. Distinguished by their gaily-painted hulls and their tan and white sails.

CONCARNEAU TUNNY BOAT

WHALING

Whale hunters have existed for hundreds of years. Early hunters 'fished out' the Bay of Biscay in the 14th century and during the 16th and 17th centuries whalers operated in northern waters around Iceland and Spitsbergen. In the early colonial days in New England whales were hunted by various methods and over the next 200 years America became the centre of whale hunting, developing purpose-built whaling barques. Martha's Vineyard and New Bedford became the home ports for many of these vessels by 1850.

NEW BEDFORD WHALER

Whaling barques were purpose-built vessels in the late 19th century. Hulls were sheathed with greenheart wood to withstand the ice wear and tear, where these ships had to operate. The hulls were deep and strong to accommodate stoves and boilers for treating blubber. Some vessels of 500 tons had auxiliary steam power.

Six to eight whaleboats carried on davits did the actual catching with hand harpoons when whales came up to blow. These boats were strong double-ended rowing boats and extremely fast, steered by a helmsman's oar over the back of the boat.

XEBEC 1750

The world xebec simply means a small sailing ship, three-masted, originally of Turkish and Arab design. The Arab and French types were originally both lateen-rigged on all masts but after the middle 1700's some were rigged with lateen and square sails on extended masts. These vessels were called polacre-rigged. The Algerian coast corsairs were great experts at sailing these ships which were usually armed with between 20 and 30 guns. Rowing benches could be set between gun positions and were often used to great advantage in their pirating fleets when dealing with sluggish square-rigged merchantmen.

Other Mediterranean nations such as Spain and Portugal had their own versions of this craft. These armed xebecs were approximately 20 to 35 metres in length and were considered very fast sailers in most conditions, outsailing square-riggers of the time. The underdeck was acutely curved, 'turtleback' or barrel-shaped to facilitate fast top-deck drainage. The working deck above had many gratings.

YACHT 1650

The illustration shows a Dutch Admiralty yacht. These were vessels of pleasure developed by the Dutch and used originally to convey important members of state between various countries. With useful shallow draft, vessels could be used on the many inland waterways of Holland. Strongly built with leeboards and a single mast carrying a square topsail, fore-and-aft sail on the lower mast, the yacht was also used in the Dutch Navy as a tender or dispatch vessel. The wealthy families in Holland used smaller versions like their carriages to be towed or sailed around the waterways and canals. A towpath in Dutch is *jacht-pad*. In England the yacht was introduced after the restoration of Charles 11. Holland presented him with the 'Mary' of 100 tons, armed with 8 guns. Charles became an enthusiastic yachtsman, developing other vessels that eventually discontinued the leeboard. Yachting clubs developed in the 18th century and have developed to this day helped by Royal patronage.

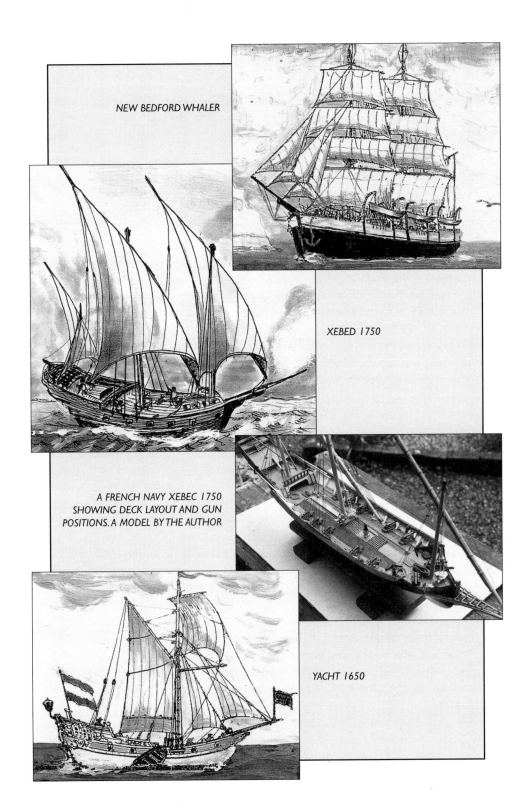

NEW BEDFORD WHALER

XEBED 1750

A FRENCH NAVY XEBEC 1750 SHOWING DECK LAYOUT AND GUN POSITIONS. A MODEL BY THE AUTHOR

YACHT 1650

SMALL SAILING SHIPS, BOATS & CRAFT

SAILING BARGES

No other wooden sailing vessel in Great Britain has survived for so long into this century. The barge is probably one of the strongest hull forms ever evolved, the shape and the gear of these sturdy craft seem to belong to a different family altogether from other sailing boats.

Sailing barges, as we know them developed from a box-like craft, flat-bottomed and used on rivers and estuaries in the 18th century. These early load carriers, not unlike latter day lighters, were entirely open craft. It was not until 1810 that decking and large hatch openings appeared.

By 1840 the wedge-shaped swimhead bow was superseded by the straight stem. The transom stern was developed after 1860 and these vessels began to look very much like those occasionally seen today, owned by enthusiasts and clubs.

Sailing matches in the 1860s developed a need and gave incentives for the development of faster hull shapes and by the mid 1890s these new craft were being used well beyond just river and estuary limits.

The main building centres were in the southeast coastal areas of England. Places such as Ipswich, Harwich, Malden and Rochester were some of the coastal towns where building yards flourished. The Rivers Thames and Medway were also important barge-building areas. Coastal barges traded across the North Sea to Europe and as late as the 1930s large schooner-rigged barges went as far afield as British Guyana in South America.

They came in all sizes. Big coastal sea-going barges had wide decks and small hatches for safety's sake. In safer waterways the river and estuary barges had a narrower beam but larger hatches, making cargo handling an easier task. Hatch coamings were usually 12in. high on river barges but up to 24in. on the larger sea-going barges. These differences and others help in recognising the various types of barges.

Barge-type vessels used various sail plans, but the economical main spritsail with a mizzenmast sail, which was either mule-rigged, or sprit-rigged was favourite. Crews for this type of rig could be reduced to the bare minimum. A captain and mate was usual with perhaps an extra hand or more when sea trips were undertaken around the coastal areas.

It is rare to find any two barges exactly the same in every detail because plans were rarely drawn. The foreman shipwright would take off all his measurements from a half model - which was the general practice - the rest depended on the eye of the craftsmen.

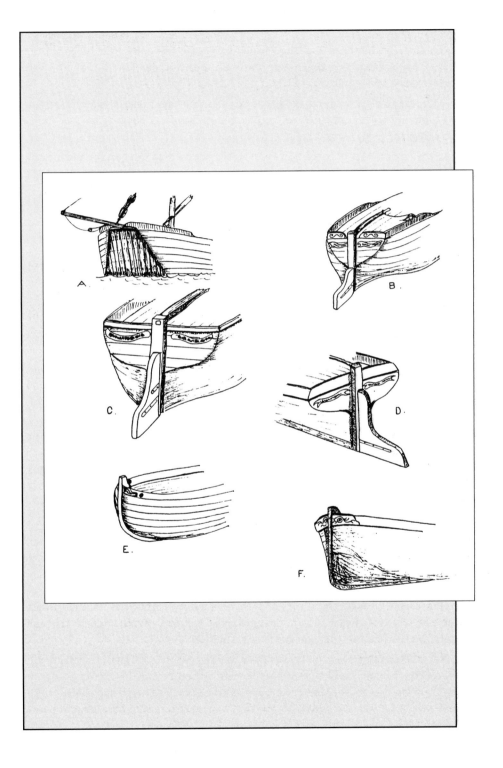

The five main types of barge - Thames coastal barge, Thames river barge, the Stumpy barge, the Humber keel and the Norfolk wherry were not the only types. The Bridgwater barge, the Teign keel, the Fenland barge, the Rye and Lamar barge and the Langston barge from the Chichester harbour area to mention just a few were particular types of their areas.

In Europe, especially in Holland, the barge came in many sizes and of different designs. Barge types are still in use today on large rivers in Europe as dumb lighters or motor barge carriers.

The following drawings of barge bows and sterns are an indication to age and in some instances the place of construction.

A) Swimhead and budget stern. The punt-shaped ends of the vessel were similar, late 17th and early 18th century, up to about 1850.

B) An early transom type, small and narrow, 1860s.

C) A later type of transom, broader and taking on the shape of the type still seen today.

D) A transom shape of about 1900.

E) A round bow reminiscent of a Dutch barge hull.

F) A concave bow by Howard of Maiden.

DUTCH STEEL BARGE 1900

At the turn of the century barges, both river and coastal types, were beginning to be constructed of steel. This enabled hull designs to be more graceful resulting in faster hull shapes. The photo illustration shows this new type of steel barge having arrived from Holland and able to come several miles inland to a town quay to unload. The main rig, although the traditional sprit, has a very long mizzen mast, a mule mizzen, heavier than the sprit mizzen looking more ketch-rigged than sprit-rigged.

HUMBER KEEL

A flat-bottomed Yorkshire vessel carrying about 100 tons. One large long hatch occupied most of the deck space. The single mast in a tabernacle supported a large square sail occasionally with a topsail. All running rigging was of wire, controlled by hand winches. Stern rails were supported on extended timbers. Some River Trent vessels were the largest, 75-80ft. long, setting a lugsail on a mizzenmast. The average length was about 60ft. with 15ft. beam and 7ft. draught. Large leeboards were fitted to the wall-sides of this bluff-bowed rounded-stern cargo carrier.

Another load carrying vessel of similar rig is the St. Lawrence Barge of Canada, some-times called a bateau. These blue-painted vessels carried timber down river to ocean-going ships for export. The difference between the Yorkshire barge and the Canadian craft is that in Canada the mast is rigged with two square sails of equal size. The bow and stern have a transom shape. Size between 100-150ft. long.

NORFOLK WHERRY

RIVER CLASS BARGE

DUTCH STEEL
BARGE 1900

HUMBER KEEL

NORFOLK WHERRY

The Norfolk wherry, working on the Norfolk Broads, was a shallow, usually clincher-built boat of 55ft. long and a wide beam of 16ft. One long cargo hatch from stern to just abaft of the single mast gave little deck space. One large loose-footed square-headed gaff sail was the only means of propulsion except for sweep oars used to negotiate certain manoeuvres. The mast was normally stepped with its weighted heel on deck supported by a lutchet, similar to a tabernacle, to enable mast lowering to deck for negotiating low bridges. A distinguishing feature was a white-painted prow area.

RIVER CLASS BARGE

Similar in general lines to the coastal barge but slightly smaller and in some cases narrower by comparison. The mizzenmast and sail is smaller than the coastal barge and is usually carried further aft, sometimes stepped on the rudderpost, the sheet rope being led to the rudder blade top. It has no bowsprit, the mainmast has a top mast.

The working ground was usually the Thames and Medway and some broad inland waters and coastal stretches. Approximate size varied but 80ft. long by 18ft. beam was common. The illustration shows a small vessel of about 45ft. long and beam of 13ft.; she carries a triangular staysail at her bow.

'STACKY' BARGE

The name 'stacky' was a bargeman's name for barges carrying hay and straw. Because of the lightweight of the cargo it was possible to stack to a considerable height from hold to well above deck level. Journeys were usually made on rivers and inland waterways. A member of the crew standing on the stack giving directions to the helmsman aided steering.

'STUMPY' BARGE

Much of the equipment and deck arrangements found on other British barges was the same on the 'stumpy'. The main difference was that the Thames and Medway stumpy had a stout pole mast in a tabernacle but no topmast or bowsprit. Some vessels of this class had no mizzenmast. The sail was the usual sprit type with triangular foresail and leeboards were usually fitted. Their smaller size enabled them to navigate the more narrow inland waterways. Early 'stumpies' had swimhead bows. This type of barge was considered a rather inferior class of vessel.

THAMES COASTAL BARGE

A ruggedly built boat, larger than the Thames 'River' class, built originally for working the east and south coastal areas of Britain and Continental ports. A heavy main and top-mast carried the usual sprit-sail and boom, the butt end kept to the mast bottom with heavy snotter chain and band. A long stout Oregon pine bowsprit, the average length 25ft. on 120-150 ton barges, was kept in place with a gammon iron and inboard post. Bobstay tackle supported and strengthened the bowsprit. The mizzen was also sprit-rigged but some vessels later favoured the mule mizzen, a heavier and taller rig surviving from the ketch rig. Most barges carried leeboards controlled with crab winches amidships.

'STACKY' BARGE

'STUMPY' BARGE

THAMES COASTAL
BARGE

BAGHLA

The largest member of the dhow type was used as a fishing vessel, freight-carrier and warship from the 16th century onwards. The rounded hull had a sharply raked bow projecting well forward. The stern poop area was usually fitted with windows and on the warship types and pirate vessels light cannon and carronades were carried on the single deck with bulwarks pierced for this ordnance. Some of these vessels used false gunports painted under the true ports to improve their threatening appearance. The sails were of dhow type on mainmast and smaller mizzen and some vessels would rig a small third mast, stepped right aft with a lateen sail for use in fair weather. Tonnage was approximately 400.

BANCA

In the Philippine Islands the natives of the Moro tribe used this outrigger dugout in pearling and fishing. It had a high tripod mast supporting a large square sail with a light yard at the head and an even lighter cane boom at the foot of the sail. This was tilted as in the illustration giving the craft great speed in favourable conditions. Sails were usually colourfully decorated.

BAWLEY

A smallish cutter-rigged estuary and coastal fishing vessel or oyster dredger working around the southeast coast of Britain. Rochester, Whitstable, Leigh-on-Sea, Harwich and the Thames Estuary were the main areas. Shrimping and whitebait fishing in season was another job suited to this craft. The mainsail is set loose-footed on a long gaff and could be brailed up, sprit-fashion. A long bowsprit with jib and staysail completed the rig.

BEURTMAN

A small Dutch cargo vessel in use at the beginning of the 19th century. Like many Dutch boats she is built in the strong fashion of the barge but has a swept up stern and lozenge-shaped lee-board. Sizes varied but 30 to 50 ft. in length was standard. Sprit-rigged with one or two headsails was the rig of this somewhat tubby vessel.

BLANKENBURG BRIG

Belgian fishermen used these lugger-rigged vessels around the mouth of the Schelde in northern Europe during the 17th and 18th century. The two masts, one at the extreme bow, forward-raked, carried conventional lugsails except for the main sail foot that was stiffened with a curved boom. A bridle was attached to the mainsail luff edge. The lee-boards on this vessel were long and narrow. The hull, carvel built, came to a rounded point at bow and stern. A deep rudder, tiller-controlled, was attached to the swept-up stern.

BAGHLA

BANCA

BAWLEY

BEURTMAN

BLANKENBURG BRIG

53

BRAGGOZZO

A vessel of the Adriatic region used by the Venetians on the southern inlet of the Lagoon and fishermen along the Dalmatian coast as a medium-sized fishing and cargo vessel. Heavily-built and flat-bottomed with shallow draught these hulls had considerable beam and lengths varied between 28 to 45ft.. long. Although bluff-bowed vessels could sail quite fast in a good breeze with their two sails that were a cross between a lugsail and lateen shape, stiffened with thin booms and yards top and bottom. As all Mediterranean boats they were very colourful.

CAIQUE

A term usually associated with fishing boats of the Eastern Mediterranean. The term was used very loosely so exact descriptions are difficult. In the 17th and 18th centuries these vessels were used by Turkish and Cossack corsairs as half-galleys. In the 19th century the term caique described a galley/shallop type, also a small Turkish single-masted coaster that rigged both square sails and a lateen yard and sail on a single mast. The Turkish term is kaik and could describe a boat or skiff propelled by one or two oarsmen used in Turkish waters, it also describes a Sultan's barge.

The sail plans were various. Two-masted vessels had balanced lugsails set on opposite sides of each mast, some had a balanced lug foresail and a gaff mainsail and others two gaff sails. A feature of most hulls was the pronounced sheer and high-angled bowsprit. Carvel built, the average size of late 19th and early 20th century boats was 50ft. long with a 10 to 12ft. beam.

Nowadays the word caique can describe a great variety of sailing or motorised vessels used in and around the Greek Islands and eastern Mediterranean. The illustration shows a large type of fishing boat.

NORTH AMERICAN CANOE

Canoes were being made well before America and Canada were colonised. Sizes and shapes were based on tribal tradition and the local conditions where these craft were used. When the frames were set up the covering could be of animal skin or bark from the paper birch tree. A canoe of 20ft. long would have a beam of about 40 in. and could carry almost half a ton. A 30ft. canoe could carry about 25 men. The early settlers and traders soon appreciated these useful craft and many were built for cargo carrying and the fur trade using the same system of building used by the local tribes.

CAPE COD CATBOAT

The American catboat probably developed in the New York area. By 1850 this type was common there. One of the local builders supplied two of his boats to England where the sailing qualities were much admired by yachtsmen. These English vessels were called 'una-boats', in Germany bobfisch.

The catboat developed from the old centreboard sloop, a type designed to work with mainsail only. With no use for head sails the mast moved forward. Boat enthusiasts used cats in smooth water but fishermen of the period used them for much of their fishing along the Cape shore.

BRAGGOZZO

CAIQUE

NORTH AMERICAN CANOE

CAPE COD
CATBOAT

FRENCH CHASSE-MARÉE

During the 18th century many coasters adopted the lug rig based on a design of fishing vessels. During the Revolutionary and Napoleonic Wars 1793-1815 these luggers were used by the French largely for smuggling and privateering. Although still called Chasse-Marée, a refined version became an armed lugger used by the navies on both sides of the Channel. Chassse-Marée literally means tide chasers.

BALTIMORE CLIPPER

The word clipper is a generic term denoting types of very fast sailing ships.

The need for fast sailing ships that were seaworthy and economical to run at the beginning of the 1800s produced a whole family of craft on both sides of the Atlantic. The English cutter, the French lugger and the American clipper were these medium-sized vessels. The Baltimore clippers were used for many purposes, both legal and otherwise. One such craft, the American Navy's 'Lynx' built at Baltimore in 1812 was captured by the British in a skirmish in 1813. She was taken into the Navy under the name of 'Musquidobit', as illustrated here. The Admiralty's plans of her in 1816 showed a length of 94ft. 7in., a beam of 24ft. and a depth of hull of 10ft. She weighed 223 tons with 6 to 8 guns carried on a single open deck.

These clippers built in Maryland and Virginia became famous during the war of 1812 as blockade-runners and privateers. They were later notorious for slave-running.

COBLE

The coble type is one of the most distinctive working boats of Britain in its original form and was mainly carvel-built with a marked sheer, considerable tumblehome with a raked, narrow transom. As a fishing boat of the northeast coast of Britain the normal equipment consisted of a mast carrying a narrow dipping lugsail with larger versions fitted with bowsprit and mizzenmast. Three pairs of oars were usual worked on iron rings over single thole pins. The hull's flatish bottom went forward into a deep forefoot made slightly deeper than the keel to balance the very deep rudder; this gave the boat a good grip to windward. The coble was launched mainly from the beaches, bow to seaward and stern to beach on return, backed in by oars.

The Scottish coble has a flat bottom and is an open rowing boat from the west coast of Scotland used for salmon fishing. It bears little resemblance to the English type, except in its name.

Grace Darling and her father used cobles for their rescue boat.

An old coble of the large type completely renovated with bowsprit and two masts, seen here at Bude, Cornwall.

FRENCH CHASSE-MARÉE

BALTIMORE CLIPPER

COBLE

H371

CORACLES

A very ancient skin boat mentioned in the early writings of Timaeus who died about 256 BC When the Romans landed in Britain they found the local people using skin boats on rivers and inland waterways. The Welsh called them corwg or cwrwgl; this name was corrupted into the English coracle. The Welsh made a seagoing version called a corwc, this larger vessel was no doubt related to another skin boat called a curragh of Irish origin. The framework was easy to make from ash or willow strips, arched with the ends stuck into the ground until the sides and bottom were woven, weights being placed on the bottom to flatten. The Teifi coracle is still built in Wales to this day. Julius Caesar used the idea of making large skin boats in one of his campaigns in Spain, his ideas gained from his experiences in Britain.

Another similar ancient craft used on the Euphrates is called a quaffah, made round of woven basket material and coated with bitumen.

THE IRONBRIDGE CORACLE

This type was still being used in the early twentieth century on the River Severn. It was a round craft with no wickerwork but made of strips of flat, split or sawn timber.

THE TEIFI CORACLE

This Welsh river coracle is still made today. Sizes vary depending on the skin material available. Tar-covered canvas can be used though in place of the original hides. 5ft. x 3ft. and 15in. deep is an average size. A rope across the seat is used to carry the coracle on the back.

CROMER CRAB BOAT

There were many crab boats working around the southern coastal areas of Britain at the turn of the century. Norfolk, Cornwall and Devon had these small double-ended boats identified by their ports of origin. Cromer crabbers, as in this illustration, Cadgwith, Gorran Haven, Hallsand, Hope Cove, Penberth and Sherringham all had their individual boats. These were quite deep boats usually clincher-built with deep rudders, a single mast with a lugsail that could be raised when conditions were favourable. Oars were used through locks pierced in the gunwale top. Many of these were motorised in the 20th century.

BRITISH NAVAL ARMED CUTTER 1763

The cutter was a well-known rig when in 1763 thirty-one such craft were bought into the British Navy. They were very broad in proportion to their length, with an average length of just over 60ft. and a beam of 20ft. Cutters were fast and weatherly craft able to carry enormous sail areas of both square and fore-and-aft canvas on a single stout mast. The excessive beam was necessary to provide the right amount of stability. The cutter was employed mainly for auxiliary work for the naval fleet and on the preventive services against smugglers. The armaments were light and consisted of up to ten 4-pounder guns, their good speed being their main protection. Later many were widely used in the Trinity House pilot services.

THE IRONBRIDGE CORACLE

THE TEIFI CORACLE

CROMER CRAB BOAT

BRITISH NAVAL ARMED CUTTER 1763

MAN-OF-WAR CUTTER 1800

Another version of an armed cutter - in this illustration the single mast has two standard square topsails instead of one. A useful fast boat used for communication work in the Navy between the first line ships of the 1800s.

PILOT CUTTER

The cutter rig was introduced in the mid 1700s. A smallish, decked ship with one mast and a bowsprit, a gaff mainsail on a boom with a square yard and topsail on early versions, as in revenue cutters. Two head sails were usually fitted, a single jib with a stay-sail. The Pilot cutter was carvel-built with an average length of 30 to 45 ft. Many sailing enthusiasts adopted these Trinity House pilot service ships when steam pilot vessels took over at the turn of the century.

DAHABIYAH

An ancient type of Nile craft used by wealthy Egyptians and luxuriously fitted-out for travelling in great comfort in the 19th century. Napoleon's campaign in Egypt could have been responsible for the growth of European interest in travel to the area. Upgraded versions were built expressly to carry the prosperous Europeans up the Nile to Aswan. The widely-spaced masts allowed space for large covered saloon cabins with top deck accommodation for viewing the sights. The hulls were flat-bottomed to negotiate the Nile sandbanks. Sizes were various, 40-110ft. long. The vessels made for the new tourists were of the smaller size taking between eight to ten travellers in comfort. Although good sailers, these vessels were sometimes towed.

DGHAISA

An all-purpose, double-ended, harbour boat of Malta carvel-built and gaily decorated. The prow and stern finished with a swept-up prow piece continuing from a vertical stem and stern, this was sometimes scimitar shaped. Larger versions were used, like the inter-island Gozo boats called dghaisa-tal-pass and carried masts, sails and high tiller arm. A smaller working boat built as a dghaisa but with a cut-off stern and flat transom board was called a kajjik. (See farella, another 19th century Maltese craft).

DGHAISA

MAN-OF-WAR CUTTER 1800

PILOT CUTTER

DAHABIYAH

DHANGI

On the West Coast of India the dhangi worked as an Arab trading vessel. The hulls were sharp at stem and stern, the prow had a swept-up 'beak'. One feature was a strong capstan mounted on the raised poop deck. A fast sea boat capable of long trading trips. Vessels varied in size but a length of 75ft, beam of 22ft. and 100 tons weight was average.

DHOW

The term dhow describes many variations of this Arab vessel. The origins start in very early times but it was in the 15th and 16th centuries when definite information about these vessels was recorded. One or two-masted vessels, depending on size, were made up to 200 tons displacement. The typical dhow rig on fairly short masts set lateen settee sails. The dhows were for many centuries the dominant means of transport over routes along the Mediterranean and east coast of Africa to the Red Sea and Arabian Gulf. Many travelled to India and the Kenyan coast. As one would expect, slave-running and piracy feature in the history of these interesting vessels.

DORY

A simple, small flat-bottomed rowing boat associated with the coast of New England, used widely for line fishing on the Grand Banks off Newfoundland. The dory had acute sheer, sharp-sloping prow and stern, this was Y-shaped and had heavy hoisting rings attached. Because of their heavily sloped sides and thwarts that would detach, these boats nested together on board the fast Gloucester schooners. Several boats spread out around the parent craft with two fishermen per dory. Fishing was usually brisk when cod were running, filling the boat every twenty minutes or so. Dories would return to the schooner and be expertly winched on board, emptied in seconds and dropped back in the water for more fishing. Sizes varied slightly between 15 and 19ft. long.

FARELLA

A robust 19th century Maltese fishing boat that was also used as a cargo vessel in trade with Tunis. These gaily-painted boats used a small spinnaker-like boom extending from the tack of the small headsail. The mainsail was supported at the peak with a slender sprit boom, the heel of which was away from the mast butt. Washboards increased the freeboard on the longer sea journeys. The lengths of hull were about 18 to 24ft.

FELUCCA

A Spanish and Portuguese sailing vessel that was used in many forms in various coasting trades of the Mediterranean. It was a fast sailer both running and when beating to windward. Most feluccas were not very large vessels, lateen-rigged on one or two masts and occasionally with a small mizzenmast. Small feluccas were worked with 6 or 8 oars and in some situations sails and oars were used simultaneously.

The sea-going types have disappeared but they can still be found as one and two-masted versions on many eastern Mediterranean rivers and estuaries like the Nile.

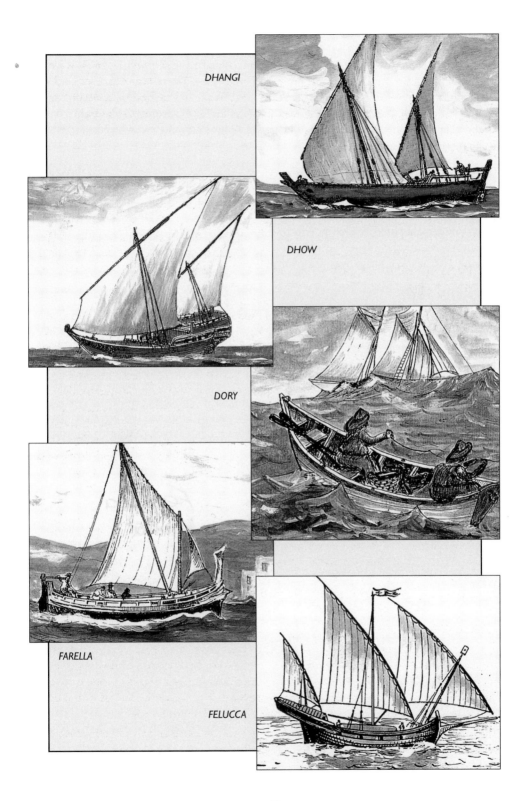

DHANGI

DHOW

DORY

FARELLA

FELUCCA

63

FIFIE

The Scottish fifie fishing boat bears some resemblance to the Cornish lugger. It is like a 'skaffie' but has a straight vertical stem and stern post. These craft were originally open but in the mid 19th century decks were fitted. Two masts carried lugsails with narrow tops, the main mast set quite forward and the shorter mizzenmast stepped in front of the tiller position just behind the hold covers. As was common with lugger mizzens, a light jigger boom extended the mizzen clew.

MERSEY FLAT

This working boat was used mainly for coastal trading in the 19th century. They were larger than the Weaver flats with finer lines. As a coaster the vessel had a small fore hatch and a main hatch divided in two by a narrow transverse space. The masts were in tabernacles for the inland and river journeys. Dimensions were approximately 78ft. long by 21ft. beam. Tonnage was just over 100.

WEAVER FLAT

This flat-bottomed sailing barge was a vessel used on the Rivers Weaver and Mersey in the 19th century. Their cargoes were mainly coal and salt. The hulls in the early part of the 19th century had square sterns but later the sharp stern was introduced. The 6ft. hold had a 60 ton capacity. Hull length was approximately 62ft. by 17ft. beam.

WARSHIP'S GALLEY

The galley was a rowing and sailing ship's boat carried by 19th century warships; they were also shore and harbour boats. Similar to the gig but larger, measuring approximately 32ft. by 5ft. 11in. beam driven by large lugsails on two masts giving a sail area of approximately 270 sq.ft. In reasonable weather her capacity was 28 persons. They could be used as liberty boats for the crews of the late 19th century navy.

WARSHIP'S GALLEY

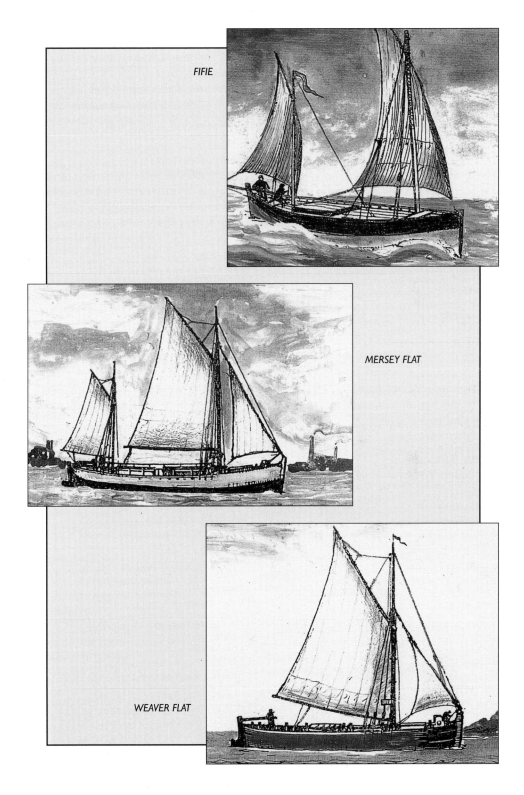

FIFIE

MERSEY FLAT

WEAVER FLAT

65

GUNDALOW

It is hard to believe that this type of river barge was American, sailing on the Merrimac River in New Hampshire with a high curved bow sweeping up canoe fashion, a short mast sporting a large lateen-type sail that would look more at home in Arab waters. The sail yard had a heavily-weighted end to balance the high sail. There was another offshore fishing schooner of Maine with a characteristic high stern called a gundalow.

GYASSA

Sometimes called gyassi or gaiassa, this trading vessel of the Upper Nile was flat-bottomed with a broad square stern and huge rudder. It was not unlike the nugger, another boat of the lower Nile. One, and sometimes double-masted, the gyassa spreads a very large main lateen sail on a yard twice as long as the vessel itself and a smaller one on the second mast. It was used mainly as a Nile cargo boat, running up river before the prevailing wind, while returning on the river drift towards the sea. The swept-up bows have a purpose - they avoided sticking into the soft banks of the river if rammed.

BRIGHTON HOG BOAT

The Brighton 'hoggie', a south coast English fishing vessel of the 18th and 19th centuries seems to have inherited a little of the Dutchman. A very broad-beamed boat with leeboards and a modified sprit boom rooted two-thirds up the main mast, gunter fashion. A heavy vertical transom and wide bilge keels gave the vessel great stability for fishing in the English Channel. The mizzen spritsail mast tight up on the transom was extended with a jigger pole.

HODY

A Bombay fishing boat with a dhow-type sail. The single mast was raked forwards and the hull was fitted with forward washboards. A crew of about 12 men worked the nets and rowed the boat on occasions, using thole pins in the gunwale to secure the oars.

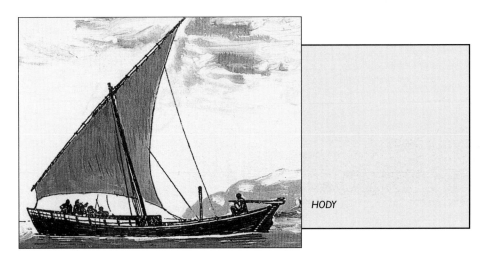

HODY

GUNDALOW

GYASSA

BRIGHTON HOG BOAT

HOOGARTS (Hoogaars)

This distinctive yet obvious Dutchman could be seen in the Walcheren Island area of Holland in the 1800s; a smallish mussel and shrimping vessel with a flatish bottom aft. Sturdy lee-boards were fitted to a strong hull made from particularly broad planks. An open well with stove fitted was part of the boat's equipment, used to boil the catch before returning to port. In most cases they were sprit-rigged.

GALWAY HOOKER

A small cutter-rigged craft of the west coast of Ireland. Most vessels had a short fore-deck with the rest of the hull left open apart from a locker seat in the square stern. The hull had a certain amount of tumblehome and is fitted with wash strakes. Another feature of this Irish vessel was the custom of tarring and greasing the sails. Turf and peat were two of the main cargoes of these vessels.

JAEGT

An ancient type of Norwegian coaster, now virtually obsolete. The true jaegt was a direct descendant of the Viking long ship. These vessels were active from the 14th to the 19th century. Their main use was to bring down dried fish and fish caught around the Lofoten Islands to Bergen and on return takes coffin boards to the various ports en route. Another use was to provide a setting for wedding parties when the poop area of the deck was elaborately decorated as an arbour for the happy couple to sit in. A large square mainsail and sometimes a square topsail were rigged on the single mast. When one sail only was used, a bonnet extending it was laced to the foot.

HOOGARTS (Hoogaars)

GALWAY HOOKER

JAEGT

69

THE JUNK

We always associate the word 'junk' with China and the Far East. The name comes from the Portuguese junco, adapted from the Javanese djong ship. These flat-bottomed vessels are of ancient design with one to five masts. The lug-type sails were made of matting or various kinds of woven cloth and stiffened with horizontal battens. With high sterns and squared-off bows with no recognised stem, the beam of the vessel was broadest one third of the length from aft. The broad stern carried a large deep rudder, which is lowered below the depth of the bottom. The sizes varied considerably. Some of the largest were built at least as big as 18th and 19th century western square-rigged ships with dead-weights of three and four thousand tons. These very large ocean going trading junks would sail the Western Pacific journeying as far as the Philippine Islands.

The design has stood the test of time with some small vessels nowadays looking very much like those of two hundred years ago. Modern Chinese motor junks are a familiar sight in many Far Eastern ports and harbours. They make excellent homes for the land-starved populations of this part of the world.

The following descriptions of the various types of junk cover only a few of these odd yet interesting vessels.

One man stands alone for his amazing journey in a homemade vessel called 'Liberdade' using a three-masted junk rig. Captain Joshua Slocum's ship 'Aquidneck' was wrecked in Brazilian waters in 1887. With only a few tools rescued from his wrecked ship he and his wife, son and mate built a flat-bottomed dory cum coastal sampan measuring 35ft. long with a beam of 7ft. and draught of 2ft., her weight 6 tons. The boat's bottom was made of local ironwood and the rest from cedar. The mainmast was spruce, the foremast and mizzen of local hardwood. Three junk sails of cotton duck made by his wife were stiffened with bamboo battens. Setting sail, after a few trials, from Paranagua in Brazil in July 1888 they reached Washington DC, USA in December 1888, a journey of 5,510 miles in 53 days of actual sailing - proof enough of the efficiency of a junk rig.

ICHANG RIVER JUNK

A shallow draught vessel designed for working the upper reaches of the Yangtze river. A small deckhouse to provide some shelter for the helmsman was usually set in the stern area. The foremast is raked forward whilst the main and mizzen is almost vertical. The usual junk lugsails are set although most craft carried long oars called 'yulows'.

JAPANESE JUNK

Although a junk, this Japanese version of the craft is different from the Chinese junk. The sails are unbattened and the sail seams are roped to take the weight of sail and provide some stiffness. The open stern has a long tiller with tackles. The two small sails in the forward area assist steering. On the heavy stem post a narrow bound tassel is hung as the sign of a trading vessel.

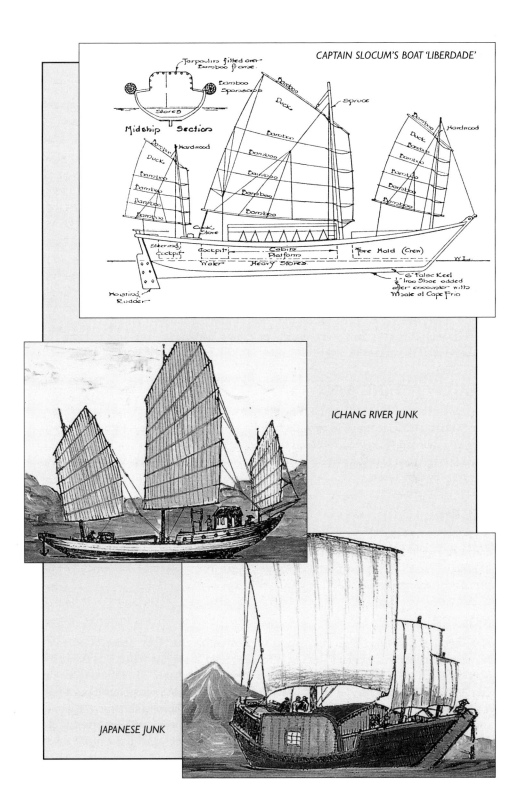

CAPTAIN SLOCUM'S BOAT 'LIBERDADE'

ICHANG RIVER JUNK

JAPANESE JUNK

MANDARIN JUNK

Ceremonial events were very important in China. High personages could travel in beautifully accommodated junks, elaborately decorated. These vessels were shallow draught craft propelled on occasions by large sweep oars. The two masts were set well forward giving ample room for the sumptuous stateroom from amidships to stern.

PEKING RIVER JUNK

This is one of the single-masted junks, very beamy, flat-bottomed, drawing only a foot or so of water. The waterways from Peking to Nanking and Shanghai had many shallows and rapids. In difficult water a bowman with a long sweep stood ready to assist direction.

SHANTUNG JUNK

This trading vessel operated between the Yellow Sea ports down to Shanghai. The hull is whale-backed with a similar bulge found on western 'turret-deck' steamers of the period. It had five masts, three set on the hulls centre line and two smaller ones set on the extreme port side. Sails were usually of canvas, battened in the junk fashion. The dimensions of these vessels were 150ft. long by 32ft. beam.

SWATOW FISHING JUNK

This type of sea-going trawler junk originated from the Formosa channel area. A very sturdy boat, well-built and able to withstand heavy weather. The long deep rudder was hung into a broad stern-well, recessed to take the rudder far below the keel. The nets, when fishing, were usually towed between two vessels. Approximate dimensions were 50ft. long by 14ft. beam.

KOLEH

A fishing boat of the Straits Settlements, as it was known. A native craft, long, narrow and sprit-rigged with jib sail, some boats had small mizzens. A number of these boats used to be raced off Singapore when the crews were increased to 14 or 15 men. Length of hull was approximately 30ft.

KOSTER

A Swedish boat named after the island of Koster on the west coast of Sweden. Nineteenth century smugglers were said to have used these clincher-built vessels the hulls of which were double-ended and measured approximately 20- 35ft. long. It was considered a good sea boat in skilful hands and eventually found respectability as a fishing boat and later as a yacht. The vessel was decked having a forehatch, large well amidships and a small square cockpit aft. The high mast, gaff and the topsail supported at the head with a topsail yard must have been useful in catching the wind in the high banked inlets from the sea in that part of the world.

MANDARIN
JUNK

SHANTUNG JUNK

SWATOW
FISHING
JUNK

PEKING RIVER
JUNK

KOLEH

KOSTER

73

LAKATOI

This native-built craft from the New Guinea area is made from two dugout canoe hulls joined by a platform. The boat's length was approximately 35-40ft., the hulls held about 5-6ft. apart. The crab claw shaped sails have a purpose apart from giving deck space, sea breakers could flow over and through the vessel unimpeded by the lower sails made usually of matting strips.

CORNISH FISHING LUGGER

The Cornish version of the lugger was used mainly for pilchard fishing. The sail rig consisted of a dipping lugsail on the mainmast with a standing lug on the mizzen. A long outrigger, fitted at the stern, helped to spread the mizzen sheet. The lugger rig is said to have originated in France (logger or lougre) and developed from the late 17th century into a great variety of craft being used for fishing and the coastal trades where the rigs increased weatherliness over the square rig, giving some advantage when working tides.

FLUSHING PILOT LUGGER

A long, open boat rigged with mainmast almost amidships and mizzenmast stepped close up to the transom with outrigger boom to extend the sheet. These vessels looked similar to early English luggers of the south coast but were faster sailers, a necessity when taking the pilot out to ships negotiating the Schelde in Holland.

GRAVELINES LUGGER

This early type of French lugger or lougre, as called in France, was one of the many ships using this rig in the 18th and 19th centuries. She was a small boat to be fitted with three masts but they were strongly built with straight sides and heavy transom well suited for fishing the local waters. Length of hull was approximately 60ft. The main mast sometimes carried a topsail.

HASTINGS LUGGER

This well-known south coast fishing boat can still be seen today in its modern form. Originally, it was unique among fishing vessels of the period, being fitted with an iron centreboard. The stern had evolved from a straight vertical transom into a lute stern during the second half of the 19th century, as in the illustration. In the 20th century the elliptical stern evolved where the strakes of the hull were brought up and around the stern.

These clinker-built vessels carried a dipping lugsail on the main mast, in tabernacles, with a standing lug set on the mizzenmast. The average dimensions were approximately 28ft. long x 11ft. beam. Late 19th century versions were larger and could set a jib, a main topsail and a mizzen staysail in addition to those standard sails previously mentioned. Large luggers were decked; the smaller versions were left open.

HASTINGS LUGGER

LAKATOI

CORNISH FISHING
LUGGER

FLUSHING PILOT
LUGGER

GRAVELINES
LUGGER

75

ROWING LIFEBOAT

Before the advent of reliable marine engines coastal lifeboats were rowed and when conditions allowed lugsails were raised. These sturdy double diagonal carvel-planked boats were fitted with air cases at bow and stern. Water ballast, false iron keels and hefty cork fender belts fitted just below the gunwale top gave the hull self-righting qualities. Dimensions were approximately 33ft. x 8ft. beam. Pulling on average 12 oars fitted on thole pins or in rowlocks, the crew consisted of about 15 men. At bow and stern the boats were closed in with small curved quarterdecks. The illustration shows a boat of the 1890s.

Britain is said to have been the first nation in the world to adopt an organisation for saving life at sea. The first lifeboat was built in 1760 but in 1785 a coachbuilder named Lukin converted a Norwegian yawl into a serviceable lifeboat and later a coble was also converted and used at Bamborough, Yorkshire. After much public and government discussion, Henry Greathead, a South Shields boatbuilder, built the first proper purpose-built lifeboat in 1789. In 1824 the RLNI was founded.

LORCHA

European companies in the early 19th century used these vessels in the Far East for trading, sometimes in opium. The European type hull was fitted with Chinese junk sails for simple handling by native crews. This lug-rigged trader had the usual battened canvas sails and was a fast sailer. The lorcha is believed to have originated at Macao when the Portuguese first settled it.

MAHAILA

One of the largest types of native vessel working on the river between Baghdad and Basrah. These vessels had a very pronounced sheer and a mast with a forward rake carrying the usual lateen sail. The hulls were shallow draught with a stern higher than the bows. The angled stern post supported a huge, shallow but horizontally long, rudder.

MAHAILA

ROWING LIFEBOAT 1890

ORIGINAL
GREATHEAD
LIFEBOAT

LORCHA

MARAJO FISHING BOAT

At the mouth of the Amazon river and the nearby coasts these rakish fishing boats worked the waters using nets. Their name comes from the Island of Marajo at the mouth of the great South American river. It was about 40ft. in length and gunter-rigged on a raked mast. The boom at the foot of the mainsail was very long, overlapping the stern by approximately 10ft.

MULE

The mule was a type of coble fishing boat but differs from the coble having a sharp stern. The main building areas were Filey and Scarborough in North Yorkshire. The fine stern suited the type of seas in the area, especially heavy following seas. The mule was an open boat with a single, slightly raked, mast carrying a squarish lugsail.

MULETTA

The Portuguese muletta was basically a lateen-rigged fishing trawler originating from the Tagus. The bow was exceptionally bluff with a slightly less curved stern. The hull had an almost concave bottom, this facilitated easy beaching and keeping the vessel upright. The strange assortment of sails helped to control various trawling speeds. These craft had extremely long bowsprits and an almost horizontal boom stretching out well beyond the stern. Sail areas were huge for a boat of this size in the late 1800s. An average length was approximately 50ft; crews were between 15 to 18 men.

MUMBLE BEE

A small cutter-rigged fishing vessel from the Brixham area. Her method of fishing was by beam trawling. A distinguishing feature was the large triangular foresail. The odd local name for this type of boat is said to have once been 'bumble bee' until catches started to be landed at Swansea when the name was altered to mumble bee, no doubt taken from the Mumbles, an area just south of Swansea.

PATTIMAR

This is a vessel of the Indian coastal waters between Colombo and Bombay. These boats of 100ft. long had a pronounced sheer and were usually painted red and black. The two masts raked forward carrying a dhow-type rig, a small jib sail was supported by a jib boom set at an angle.

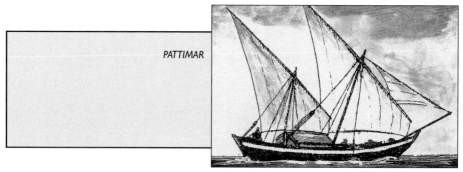

PATTIMAR

MARAJO FISHING BOAT

MULE

MULETTA

MUMBLE BEE

PETER BOAT

Thames fishermen used this spritsail-rigged boat in the 18th and early 19th centuries. Double-ended and clincher-built, these vessels worked up as far as London Bridge. An average size was 19ft. x 7ft. beam. Most carried a wet well amidships for keeping the catch fresh. A removable cabin top was carried by most of these small river-fishing boats.

ESSEX PINKY

The illustration shows a pinky of a slightly different type to the other American boats. Many of these craft were built by rule of thumb so each vessel became unique although the general class shape remained constant. In the 1820's an average size was 52ft by 13ft beam.

NEW ENGLAND PINKY

The word 'pinke' was an old European shipbuilder's term to describe a sharp-sterned vessel with a false stern, overhanging; a large sailing vessel used in the western Mediterranean in the 15th century. The American pink or pinky, however, was a seaworthy sailing craft of New England. Pinks were rigged in various ways originally but the two-masted, fore-and-aft rig became the standard. Up to about 1800 there seems to have been no real offshore fishing boat type. After the Revolution a small inshore boat was developed in Gloucester, 30-40ft. long. The sizes increased and by 1800 they were being used on the Grand Banks. The illustration shows a vessel of about 1835, 52ft. long overall by approximately 13ft. beam.

ARMED PINNACE

A ship's boat carried on large sailing warships from the 17th to 19th century. It was similar to the captain's barge but smaller, used for carrying officers ashore. The size of pinnace varied according to the rating of the warship but in general terms pinnaces were smaller and slimmer than launches. Size ranged between 24-36ft. One to three masts could be stepped and a light gun could be carried on runners up front. These boats were used for cutting-out operations during the Napoleonic wars when sailors and marines made some brave captures of enemy craft, usually at anchor and at night.

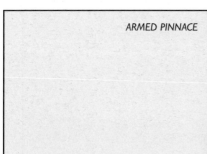

ARMED PINNACE

PETERBOAT

ESSEX
PINKY

NEW ENGLAND
PINKY

PROW

A Bombay harbour boat employed in cargo carrying. The long stern with pronounced rake was fine with the stern area widening and rounding off at the angled rudderpost. The hull was undecked except for a small area amidships for the crew to sleep and cook. The largest vessels were about 100 tons.

SAMBUK

One of the many dhow-type Arabic boats, smaller and faster than the 'baghla'. These vessels were usually roughly built with a square stern and no ornamentation. The hull was decked and the two masts support the usual eastern fore-and-aft sails. They were used mainly for carrying passengers and some freight. An iron tiller is fitted with lines to a wheel. Approximate size 64ft. by 18ft. beam and a 10ft.6in. depth of hold.

SCHOKKER

Dutch fishing vessel that evolved over six hundred years. Schokkers were originally designed for fishing the Zuidersee, the name could refer to the island of Schokland in the same area. Nineteenth century versions had a curved gaff with the sail laced to this and the mast with the foot of the sail left loose but attached to the boom at the tack and clew. A boom spar could be swung out over the ship's side for trawl nets in these later versions. A particularly heavy stem post was divided for a pulley to carry the warp to which was attached a large grapnel-type anchor. Sizes vary - hull length 45 to 52ft. with a beam of approximately 16 to 19ft.

MARBLEHEAD SCHOONER

The original American fishing schooner of the late 1700s was known as a 'heel tapper'. The stout hull had low bulwarks around the foredeck and a high raised poop deck aft, reached by a ladder from the main deck. The average size of these craft was 52ft. long, 15ft. beam and a hold depth of 7ft.6in. The rig was fore-and-aft, gaff-rigged on both masts with a long bowsprit. Just aft of the foremast a log windlass went athwartships. This was worked with handspikes to raise the anchor cables. Wooden pumps were fitted on the main deck at the break of the poop.

TRADING SCHOONERS

The first vessels called schooners are said to have been developed in America where in 1713 a vessel of this design was launched at Gloucester, Massachusetts. The name could be from the Scottish verb to scon or scoon, to skip over water like a flat stone. Whatever the name's origin, a schooner would have normally had two masts and a fore-and-aft sail rig, the main mast taller than the foremast. Originally the foremast carried a square topsail but later this was changed to a jib-headed or jackyard topsail to fill in the area above the gaff. Three-masted schooners were built and later four and five masts were developed. Some of these vessels reached great sizes like the seven-masted 'Thomas W. Lawson'. They were used both in Britain and America for coastal trading and fishing in their two and three-masted versions.

PROW

SAMBUK

SCHOKKER

MARBLEHEAD SCHOONER

TRADING
SCHOONERS

83

NEW HAVEN SHARPIE

The sharpie seems to have evolved when New Haven oystermen were looking for a cheaper type of vessel. Flat-bottomed skiff types with centreboard and triangular sails became very popular. From about 1830 to 1870 these small two-masted boats served fishermen well in the Long Island Sound. In Roslyn Long Island an Englishman developed an improved type but New Haven builders produced the true and fastest boats. Sharpies were not big boats, the majority ranged between 20 to 30 ft. During the 1870s the French adapted this type, increasing the size and beam for use in their colonies, armed with light revolving cannons. These guard boats were about 40ft. long.

SHNAIKA

The shnaika was a wooden carvel-built Russian cargo boat working in the White Sea region in the 19th century. The rig consisted of a single mast supporting a large square mainsail suspended from a yard and a narrow mizzen gaff sail on the second mast extended on a bumpkin pole over the stern. A small square spritsail was occasionally rigged under the bowsprit.

CHESAPEAKE SKIPJACK

In the Chesapeake Bay area of America a hard-chine little working boat, said to have evolved from the New Haven sharpie, was developed as an oyster boat in the 1870s. These 'diamond-bottom' craft were cheap to make and popular with amateur builders and professionals alike. Farmers near the water could indulge in a spot of oyster catching in the season with homemade skipjacks. The length of these boats varied from 28ft. upwards. The larger vessels of around 60ft. in length were used mainly in the professional oyster business. All craft of this type had raisable centreboards. The fore-and-aft sail plan consisted of a large mainsail with a boom extending well over the sloping stern. A headsail was extended on a bowsprit with bobstay. The foot of the sail was stiffened with a three-quarter-length boom.

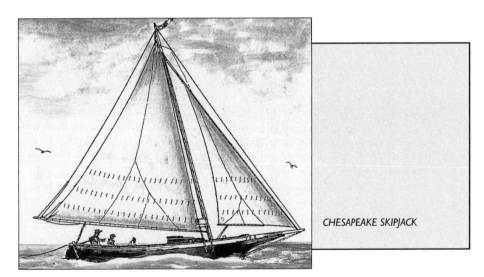

CHESAPEAKE SKIPJACK

NEW HAVEN SHARPIE

SHNAIKA

85

BERMUDA SLOOP

Early in the 17th century Jamaican shipbuilders developed an interesting type of sloop. Fast sailing craft were in great demand and the Jamaican sloop was a popular craft amongst privateers and buccaneers. Merchants used their speed to avoid capture and the Navy had a use for them also. Bermuda became an important shipbuilding island by 1700 using locally grown red cedar and it became the prime builder of an improved sloop. Their popularity reached Europe and the British navy bought these small cruisers to use in their duties at home and abroad. It is thought the Baltimore clipper schooner developed from these sloops.

FRIENDSHIP SLOOP

There were many types of sloop vessels developed from the mid 1800s in America along the Maine coastline in Muscongus Bay and in the vicinity of Friendship. Used mainly as a fast fishing vessel able to sustain maximum weatherliness under hard conditions, the keel sloop was adopted in the 1880s by schooner fishermen who were suffering from the depression in the fishing business. The carvel-built hull carried a single mast and boomed mainsail. Two headsails supported and extended on a bowsprit gave this vessel a rakish look. Sizes varied - 26ft. to 45ft. long on average.

GLOUCESTER SLOOP BOAT

These sloop boats were one of the larger types of sea-going vessels used along the American East Coast in their time. Their origins can be traced back to colonial days and their uses were many. The larger vessels carried out fishing in the North Atlantic. Built originally as a general-purpose boat they could be found in many parts including Charlestown, Boston, Salem, Beverly and Gloucester. The smaller versions resembled the friendship sloops of Maine. The sloop rig of the 1850s set two headsails, which in other parts of the world would be termed cutter-rigged. Sizes ranged from between 40 to 60ft. in length and had short quarterdecks with cabin trunk set aft.

FISHING SMACK - STEAM & SAIL

The word 'smack' is used as a generic term for all medium fishing craft irrespective of type. In the days of sail, smacks were cutter or ketch-rigged sailing vessels. In the 18th and early 19th centuries in Britain the Navy used cutter types for preventative services and as tenders to the fleet. There were many local types, the Colchester, the Whitstable smack and those used in Scottish waters to mention but a few. The single-masted cutter-rigged and larger two-masted versions, ketch-rigged, were prominent vessels that could be seen right up to the turn of the 1900s and into the early 20th century, when both steam and sail together was in use, until sail became completely redundant for fishing boats.

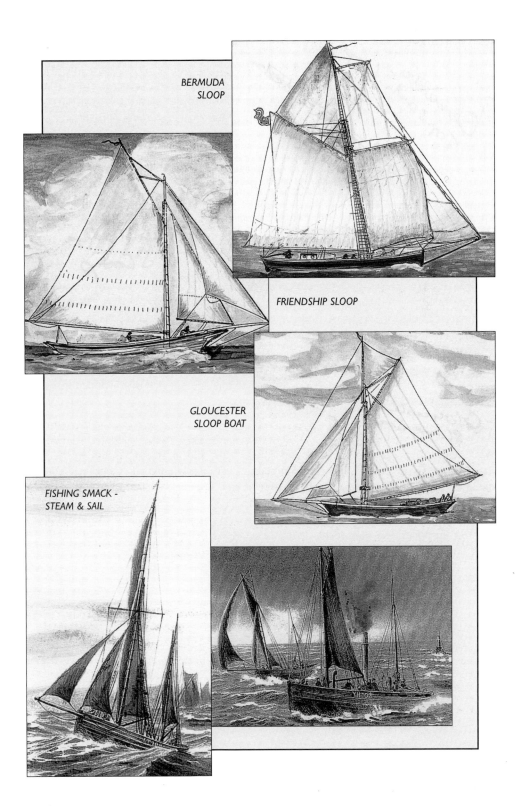

BERMUDA
SLOOP

FRIENDSHIP SLOOP

GLOUCESTER
SLOOP BOAT

FISHING SMACK -
STEAM & SAIL

WHITSTABLE OYSTER SMACK

As its name suggests, an oyster dredger fishing along the south-eastern coast of England with similar hull lines as the Colchester smack but with a heavier counter stern. The boat was cutter-rigged with a squarish topsail laced to a topsail yard the foot of which is joined to the gaff. They carried crews of 3 or 4 each working several dredgers.

SUKUNG

A sailing boat from Javanese waters, not unlike Fiji boats. The triangular sail was suspended on a curved boom and at the foot the sail was joined with another light boom. Where the two booms met at the prow of the boat a socket held the ends. Outriggers were fitted to the port side and a steering oar was hung on the same side, the mast raked forward.

TARTANA

A small Mediterranean sailing vessel with Arabian Gulf origins used in the 16th century for fishing and coastal trading. It was lateen-rigged on two masts, the foremast with considerable rake forward. Brail ropes were rigged to control sail areas. Boards fitted amidships increased the freeboard over the sheer. The hull was carvel-built.

There were many variations with some bluff-bowed. The tartan or tartane was a larger boat originating from the medieval tarette. These vessels were used by the French and Italians who developed a more refined hull and sail plan that included three foresails and large lateen mainsail on a single mast.

TJALK

A Dutch sailing vessel with a round apple bow and a lesser-curved stern; a flat-bottomed load carrier since the 19th century with a single mast in tabernacle that could be lowered. The sail had a short, straight gaff, later curved, and on the bows a bowsprit could be rigged to extend the headsail. These vessels originally had the normal barge rig of the period with jib and spritsail. The design was later adapted for yachting purposes. The tjalk yacht closely resembles an enlarged boeir, an inland craft used on waterways of the Netherlands, nowadays built of steel.

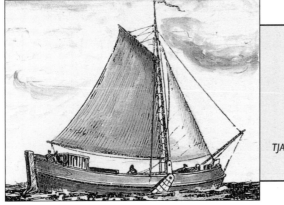

TJALK

WHITSTABLE OYSTER SMACK

SUKUNG

TARTANA

89

BRIXHAM TRAWLER

This trawler is probably one of the best known sailing boats used from around 1795 to the late 1930s. No doubt the well-sheltered fishing town of Brixham, lying in the southern corner of Torbay, sheltered from most winds but boats able to use the harbour both entering and leaving in most conditions, had a lot to do with the growth of the trawler fleets. In the Napoleonic Wars the Royal Navy, when blockading Brest, could run quickly into Torbay if westerly gales forced them off station.

After drift net herring fishing was given up around 1795 Brixham turned to trawling and over the years fleets of Brixham trawlers occupied ports all over Britain and Ireland. Brixham boats were of various sizes. In 1906 there were 220 first class boats of 15 tons registered in Brixham. After the Great War a new generation of boats were built, some over 40 tons. The last Brixham sailing trawler was built in 1927.

The evolution of the sail plan for these vessels is interesting. In Brixham lugsails replaced the original square sail in the 18th century. With the growing size of trawlers a single mast sail plan was dropped leading to a reduced mainsail on the mainmast and a mizzenmast set with gaff sail and topsails, these ketch-rigged craft were now 70ft. in length. Some vessels retained the cutter rig and were known as 'Mumble Bees' (see other details under 'Mumble Bee'). The illustration shows a ketch-rigged Brixham trawler of the early 1900s.

ULAK

This beamy double-ended craft was used as a produce barge in the Bengal area. The single mast with a sail plan of upper and lower square sails is not unlike the Humber keel rig. There is a short foredeck and poop deck, the midship part is left open but covered by a thatch roof to protect the cargo. Average size 38ft. long, 14ft. beam.

WHALE BOAT

Double ended with centreplate this fast sailing and rowing boat was the type carried by old whaling ships. It was fitted with a rudder but often steered by a single oar over the stern when the boat was rowed. A roller chock at the stem of the boat allowed the harpoon line to run freely. These lines were usually coiled into two tubs. Boats were often towed at great speed after the harpoon struck the whales they hunted, the hulls being designed for just this purpose.

DUTCH YACHT 1680

This 17th century private pleasure boat is much smaller than the Dutch State yachts. Fore-and-aft rigged yachts were used extensively on coastal and inland waterways of Holland. Early yachts were sprit-rigged, but by the middle of the century this method of sail support was discarded in favour of the half sprit or standing gaff, sometimes this yard was curved giving these vessels a distinctive Dutch look. Sizes varied but these private pleasure boats, used like the family carriage, were on average 31ft. long and carvel-built from thick planks. A small day cabin amidships made things more comfortable for the traveller. Leeboards, pivoted on both sides to decrease leeward drift, were a feature of most Dutch yachts.

BRIXHAM TRAWLER

ULAK

WHALE BOAT

DUTCH YACHT
1680

YAWL

The yawl, like the ketch, has two masts but the yawl mizzen is smaller in proportion and is stepped aft of the rudderpost. The mizzen sheet is led out on a bumpkin boom extending from the stern. The main mast is usually gaff-rigged on the original yawl with one or two headsails, the jib extended on a bowsprit. Yawl is an adaptation of the Dutch word jol, a skiff.

YOLE

This small open boat, clincher-built, came from the Shetland and Orkney islands. A beamy craft with fine lines at bow and stern reminiscent of Viking boats in hull shape and construction. The ribs joined the keel by the garboard strake of planking only. The mast was amidships and was practically vertical carrying a narrow lugsail. The skaffie lugger probably developed from the yole and the zulu lugger replaced the skaffie eventually as the larger standard working boat in Scotland.

ZULU

A broad-beamed carvel-built fishing boat peculiar to the northeast coast of Scotland. During the Zulu War 1878-9 a boat-builder named Camerson introduced this vessel in an effort to improve the local Scottish fishing types of boat. With a straight stem and a raked, pointed stern, sometimes at 45 degrees these craft largely replaced the skaffie. Hull lengths varied and were fully decked. Boats measured 54ft. x 16ft. 6in. beam.

YAWL

YOLE

ZULU

STEAM SHIPS & BOATS

The history of marine steamboats is said to have started about 1707 with the French engineer Denis Papin, who lived in Germany. He carried out his first experiments on the River Wesser. Local boatmen and river users were so incensed with this strange intrusion that they destroyed his boat and he barely escaped with his life.

In 1736 a Gloucester man named Jonathan Hulls took out a patent for his idea to fit a small boat with a pair of paddle wheels, steam-driven and positioned over the stern of the boat. In 1776 the Marquis de Jouffroy purchased one of James Watt's patent steam engines to fit a small vessel. Early experiments were not very successful but later in 1783 his boat sailed successfully on the River Saone between Lyons and the Isle de Barbe. So began a successful and fascinating story of steam propulsion on water.

In 1788 Messrs. Miller & Symington carried out practical experiments with a steamboat on Dalswinton Loch in Scotland. Miller, a wealthy Edinburgh banker, carried out these experiments with a craft that had a double hull, the boiler in one half and the engine in the other. The paddle wheel was placed between each half. The engine of only one horsepower is said to have given the boat a speed of 5 miles per hour in still water. The following year Miller bought a canal boat and fitted her out with a 12 horse-power engine built by the famous Carron Ironworks, known best for the new type of ship's cannon the Company went on to manufacture in the 19th century. The new boat managed 7 miles per hour, fully laden; the paddle-wheel was placed over the stern.

The 'Charlotte Dundas' was the next vessel to improve on their previous efforts. Built in 1802 and commissioned by Lord Dundas from Miller & Symington, the new boat towed two loaded barges of 70 tons each at a speed of 3 miles per hour on her trials. The proprietors of the Forth and Clyde Canal Company considered the wash created by the paddles would eventually destroy the canal banks so the 'Charlotte Dundas' was laid up and never used again.

The American engineer Fulton witnessed the trials of the 'Charlotte Dundas' obtaining valuable information about paddle propulsion. He started negotiations with Messrs. Boulton and Watt in Birmingham for marine engine parts, which were sent to America in 1806 to be fitted to Fulton's new steam paddler, the 'Clermont'. She was a great success sailing up the Hudson River between New York and Albany, carrying 40 passengers in 1807. The hull measured 133ft. long and had a speed of about 5 miles per hour.

The 'Clermont' was the pioneer of a steam-powered service that ultimately established the inland waterways of the United States. In England steam power was the new rage and experiments continued apace. Henry Bell, a hotel proprietor living on the Clyde, experimented with a paddle engine for his pleasure boats in the early 1800s. After negotiating with Messrs. Boulton and Watt who were rather discouraging about his

'CHARLOTTE DUNDAS'

new ideas, he approached Messrs. J. & C. Wood in 1811 resulting in an agreement for him to superintend the building of his own new vessel, the famous 'Comet'. She eventually carried passengers between Glasgow and Bell's hotel on the Clyde.

In 1816 the 70 ton 'Elise' made the first English Channel crossing under steam. She took 18 hours to make the trip. In 1819 the Americans made an important first crossing of the Atlantic from west to east. The 389 ton paddle ship 'Savannah', a barque-rigged vessel, took 29 days. She only steamed for about 80 hours on the trip, sailing for the most part.

By now there were many people involved in marine steam propulsion both in Europe and America.

The year of 1838 was famous for being the year in which continuous steam voyages were made across the Atlantic. Those vessels principally concerned were the 'Sirius', 'Great Western' and 'Royal William'. The Sirius was of 700 tons and had a 320 horse-power engine and was rigged as a brigantine. She had originally been employed as a coasting vessel between London, Bristol and Cork. She took 17 days from Queenstown to New York. The 'Great Western' was a larger vessel of 1,321 tons with a 750 horse-power steam engine, built especially for the Atlantic. Her journey time was 15 days. Her best speed accomplished a 12-day crossing.

C.S.S. 'ALABAMA' 1862

This famous American Confederate cruiser was built at the Laird Company yards of Birkenhead, England in 1862 under a contract with the Confederate agent James Bulloch. She was not the only ship bought in this fashion. Of the twelve famous major ships of the Confederate Navy six were purchased in England - namely, 'Florida', 'Alabama', 'Shenandoah', 'Georgia', 'Talahasse' and the 'Chickamauga'.

The 'Alabama' was heavily armed with six 32-pounder guns, one 7in. rifled pivot gun of 100lb. and one 8in. solid shot 68 pounder smooth bore. In 20 months she sailed many thousands of miles chasing Union shipping with great success before her sinking by the Union gunboat 'Kearsarge' June 19th 1864 just off Cherbourg, France.

EARLY ATLANTIC STEAMER 1840

After the 'Sirius' succeeded in crossing from England to America in 1838, many other medium-sized paddle-driven ships made the crossing. As time went on these crossings became more regular. This illustration shows the 'Arcadia' built for the British & North American Steam Packet Company. She carried some passengers and mail, starting in 1840.

BRITISH STEAM BATTLESHIP 1872

HMS 'Devastation' was the first British sea-going man-of-war without sails. Driven by steam powered-propellers, she went into service with two other notable battleships, the 'Thunderer' and the 'Dreadnought'. They were all completed between 1872-1875. HMS 'Devastation' as illustrated was a 9,330 ton vessel protected by a belt of 12in. thick armour on the water-line extending approximately two-thirds the length of the hull. The two gun turrets mounted at each end of the central superstructure contained two

C.S.S. 'ALABAMA'
1862

EARLY ATLANTIC
STEAMER 1840

BRITISH STEAM
BATTLESHIP 1872

12in. calibre guns, both were muzzleloaders. The turrets were made of 14in. thick steel and the ship's bow was of ram form extending a few feet just below the waterline.

HMS 'Thunderer' had similar ordnance, 'Dreadnought's' guns were a fraction larger. When fully armed the 'Devastation' had only a 4 to 5ft. freeboard making it a very wet ship in a seaway but in spite of this they were remarkable ships for the period in which they were built.

BATTLESHIP 1900

This example of a British warship was launched in 1898. It had closely spaced funnels and two equal masts, still rigged with fighting tops; rather anachronistic in view of the 12in. 50 ton guns carried as main armament together with considerable secondary armament. These ships were painted in black, white and buff and had a displacement of around 15,000 tons.

BEAM-ENGINED STEAMER

The beam engine was introduced in America about 1823 and the boats that used this engine became a very popular means of transport on the Hudson River. An overhead rocking beam suspended on a large 'A' frame was driven by a vertical steam cylinder. This power source connected with large side paddle wheels.

STEAM PADDLE BOAT 'CLERMONT'

The 'Clermont' was the first successful paddle steamer in America. In 1803 the American Minister to France, a Mr. Livingstone and an engineer called Fulton made two reasonably successful experiments on the Seine river with steam propulsion. Fulton in the same year witnessed the trials of the 'Charlotte Dundas' in Great Britain. He gained valuable information during these trials and later engaged Boulton and Watt of Birmingham to make parts for a marine engine in America. These were delivered in 1806 and the 'Clermont' was fitted out in 1807. She was a great success, running on the Hudson River between New York and Albany for a considerable time.

Some of the local Dutch farmers living on the banks of the Hudson were so alarmed one night at the noise of her paddles and the steam and sparks issuing from her funnel they fled to the woods thinking the devil was paying a visit!

THE 'COMET', FIRST CLYDE PASSENGER STEAMER

Henry Bell, a hotel proprietor living on the Clyde, experimented with paddle propulsion in the early 1800s. His discussions with Messrs. Boulton & Watt failed so he approached Messrs. J & C Wood in 1811. This resulted in the building of the 'Comet' which Bell superintended himself during construction.

The vessel was 40ft. long and had a beam of 10ft. She weighed 25 tons. The engine developed about 4 horsepower driving 2 four-armed paddle wheels. A successful passenger service developed between Glasgow and Bell's hotel on the Clyde, the first such service in Britain. An interesting feature was the funnel being used also as a mast to support a yard for the square sail she carried.

BATTLESHIP
1900

BEAM-ENGINED
STEAMER

STEAM PADDLE
BOAT 'CLERMONT'

THE 'COMET',
FIRST CLYDE
PASSENGER
STEAMER

DAY TRIP STEAMER 1890

The passenger steamer was well established by the turn of the century. Built by various organisations including railway companies, they ran routes from most ports and sea resorts along the English Channel and the north of England. Newhaven, Chatham, the Bristol Channel, Llandudno, Bridlington in Yorkshire were some of the areas covered by this popular form of transport that continued well into the 20th century.

STEAM CORVETTE

These types of vessel were among the earliest warships to be fitted with steam-driven screw propellers. This particular lightly-armed cruiser had a ram bow sweeping forward. Corvettes were flush-decked warships with a single tier of guns, smaller than a frigate.

CRUISER 1900

A first class British Naval Cruiser was a heavy ship of this period with an 11,000 ton displacement. Her armament comprised 16 guns of 6in. calibre or over; 20 smaller guns and 2 torpedo tubes, one feature was the fitting of torpedo nets. She was capable of speeds around 20 knots driven by twin screw propellers. A full complement of 600 men operated this new type of warship. Its length was 435ft. with a beam of 69ft.

'ELISE' CROSS CHANNEL STEAMER

In 1816 the 70 ton paddle steamer 'Elise' made the first ever crossing of the English Channel by a steam driven boat. She was not a large steamer, measuring only 83ft. long. The journey took 18 hours across rough seas, eventually reaching the port of Le Havre at the mouth of the Seine in France. She sailed up river to Paris to an enthusiastic welcome.

'ELISE' CROSS CHANNEL STEAMER

DAY TRIP
STEAMER
1890

STEAM
CORVETTE

CRUISER 1900

SS 'GREAT BRITAIN'

The first large iron ship built as a transatlantic liner and driven by a screw propeller system. This 322ft.. long ship was designed by Isambard Kingdom Brunel and launched at Bristol in 1843. Her steam-powered engine developed 1,500 horsepower, giving a speed of 12 knots, her displacement was 3,270 tons. The 6 masts were rigged as follows on her maiden voyage of 1845. Foremast - fore-and-aft; second mast - square-rigged; third, fourth, fifth and sixth masts were fore-and-aft. In 1846 she had her first refit when the sail rig was changed. Now with only five masts she was square-rigged on her second and third masts, all other masts were fore-and-aft.

After her maiden trip to New York in 1845 carrying 60 first class passengers and a full complement of steerage passengers she ran ashore on rocks at Dundrum Bay, lying there for 11 months. After salvage she was used as a passenger and cargo ship to Australia. After 40 years of service she was damaged off Cape Horn, ending up beached at Port Stanley in the Falkland Islands. In 1970 pontoons were fitted and she was towed to Montevideo and then on to Bristol. Now fully restored at Bristol she illustrates a fine example of iron ship building in the early days.

FIRST INTERNAL COMBUSTION SHIP

The first ocean-going ship to be fitted with the internal combustion engine was the 'Selandia'. Although this ship belongs to the 20th century, first sailing in 1912, it has been included as an important first step away from steam-driven craft. Dr. Otto Diesel perfected this engine that ran on heavy oil. The Danish vessel carried both passengers and freight. With the absence of large steam boilers these vessels were able to increase their cargo capacity, their motors being situated right aft in the ship.

JOUFFROY'S STEAMBOAT

James Watt patented his steam engine in 1769. Steam engines made by Newcomen and James Watt for pumping out mines gave many inventors ideas for using this new power in other ways. One such man, the Marquis de Jouffroy, purchased one of Watt's engines in 1776 and fitted it to a boat. His first efforts met with no success but in 1783 his boat, in the presence of 10,000 onlookers, steamed several miles on the Saone between Lyons and the Isle de Barbe. In 1788 the first successful attempts towards discovering a means of marine propulsion were carried out in Great Britain by Miller and Symington.

JOUFFROY'S STEAMBOAT

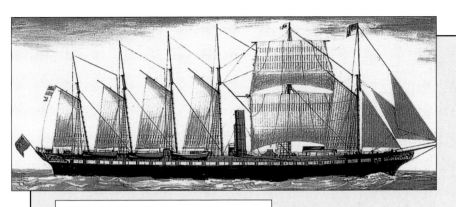

LIVERPOOL & AUSTRALIAN NAVIGATION CO

STEAM FROM LIVERPOOL TO AUSTRALIA.

THE CELEBRATED AUXILIARY STEAM-SHIP

GREAT BRITAIN,

3309 Tons, and 500 Horse-power.

CHARLES CHAPMAN, Commander,

IS APPOINTED TO LEAVE THE RIVER MERSEY,

FOR MELBOURNE AND BRISBANE

(Landing Passengers and Cargo at Melbourne, and proceeding without delay);

TAKING PASSENGERS ALSO FOR

SYDNEY, ADELAIDE, AND NEW ZEALAND,

ON SATURDAY THE 25th OCTOBER, 1873.

This magnificent and far-famed Ship has made the passage out to Melbourne in the unprecedented short time of 53 days. She affords an opportunity for Passengers to reach Australia in almost as short a time as by the Overland Route, *via* Southampton, without incurring the very heavy expenses attendant thereon, and avoiding entirely the discomfort of frequent change. Her Saloon arrangements are perfect, and combine every possible convenience, Ladies' Boudoir, Baths, etc.; and her noble passenger decks, lighted at intervals by sidoports, afford unrivalled accommodation for all classes.

FARES,

Including Steward's Fees, the attendance of an experienced Surgeon, and all Provisions of the best quality.

	TO MELBOURNE.	TO BRISBANE.
AFTER SALOON. { POOP	60 and 70 Guineas	66 and 76 Guineas
{ BELOW	55 „ 60 „	61 „ 66 „
SECOND CLASS (on Deck)	35 „ 30 „	36 „ 38 „
THIRD CLASS	25 „ 20 „	28 „ 20 „
STEERAGE	15 „ 18 „	18 „ 16 „

Children under Twelve Years, Half-price. Infants under Twelve Months, Free.

In accordance with the Passengers Act, Wines, Spirits, and Malt Liquors will be supplied on board at very moderate prices. Passengers booked to be forwarded from MELBOURNE, by the first opportunity, to SYDNEY, ADELAIDE, and HOBART TOWN, also to HOKITIKA, OTAGO, and LYTTELTON, at an extra charge of 2 Guineas Saloon, 2 Guineas other Classes. To AUCKLAND and WELLINGTON, 4 Guineas Saloon, 4 Guineas other Classes. To LAUNCESTON, 4 Guineas Saloon, and 2 Guineas other Classes.—for which separate Forwarding Tickets will be issued in Liverpool.

SS 'GREAT BRITAIN'

FIRST INTERNAL COMBUSTION SHIP

STEAM LIFEBOATS

Steam life-boats were not universally popular when they were first considered. In 1889/90 the first steam lifeboat, the 'Duke of Northumberland' completed long and extensive trials and was put on station at Harwich, later New Brighton, Holyhead and finally at Dover. These new steam powered boats were heavy vessels and could only operate from good harbours where boilers and engines could receive expert maintenance not available on slips and beaches where many lifeboats were used.

The screw-propellers of these new boats were vulnerable to damage and a system of jet-propulsion was experimented with. Finally the screw-propellers were protected by a new hull design with deep grooved recesses in which the shaft and propeller were situated. There were only 6 steam lifeboats ever in use at the same time until the introduction of the internal-combustion engine in the 20th century.

PASSENGER LINER 1890

First class passenger liners although built of steel still carried the traditional two or three masts with square sail even though they had strong compound steam engines capable of driving the ship at 18 knots or more. Some were quite large: 500ft. long with a 57ft. beam. 7,500 tons.

IRON-CLAD MONITOR CLASS

In the American Civil War (1861-65) the navies of the North and South adopted a new kind of warship, heavily armoured with iron and steel plating covering the gun deck.

The name 'Monitor' was given to one of the first such vessels, built in New York by John Ericsson in 1862. The USS 'Monitor' arrived in Hampton Roads later that year shortly after the CSS 'Virginia' (ex 'Merrimack') had sunk the Northern States USS 'Cumberland'. On 9th March the first iron-clad battle took place between the USS 'Monitor' and the CSS 'Virginia' with completely inconclusive results. The illustration shows the 'Virginia' ram ship constructed out of the old USS 'Merrimack', 275ft. long and 51ft. beam with a 24ft. draft, she displaced around 4,600 tons.

THE FIRST MONITOR WARSHIP 1862

In an age when decoration and embellishment were considered a necessary part of what was manufactured, the invention of the first monitor by John Ericsson of New York must have looked to sailors of the time like a plank of wood floating on water with a cotton reel standing in the middle. These iron and steel-clad vessels, some with revolving turrets, others that were converted from existing vessels, formed part of the war fleets on both sides in the American Civil War. For example the monitor, USS 'Onondaga' was one of 5 built by the Union with double turrets, 226ft. long and armed with two 15in. and two 8in. guns. A sun canopy was sometimes rigged over the turret as in this illustration.

As a matter of interest the word monitor, came from a phrase in a letter to the Secretary of the Navy about Ericsson's design - "The impregnable and aggressive character of this structure will admonish the leaders of the Southern Rebellion.......... The ironclad intruder will thus prove a severe monitor to those leaders".

STEAM LIFEBOATS

PASSENGER
LINER 1890

IRON-CLAD
MONITOR CLASS

THE FIRST
MONITOR
WARSHIP 1862

COASTAL PASSENGER PADDLE STEAMER

Paddle steam propulsion had few rivals for the first fifty years of the 19th century. Paddle steamers are no longer made although a number were used at Dunkirk in 1940. There are one or two still used during the summer holiday season on the south coast of England as excursion steamers like the PS 'Waverley'. The illustration shows a turn of the century paddle steamer. This type of vessel lasted well into the 20th century after refits, with many still making coastal excursions after the Second World War.

MISSISSIPPI PASSENGER STEAMER

A specially designed vessel for carrying travellers on the Mississippi River. With little freeboard and a shallow draft this enabled the embarkation and disembarkation of passengers on to low moorings. The fancy smokestack and elaborate superstructure were features of these vessels operating in the 19th and early 20th centuries. Gangways up front were suspended over the bows. There was competition between boats resulting in keen races where they attained considerable speed. Many of these boats had 3 decks with night cabins and saloons for the long distance traveller.

FRENCH RAMSHIP

Another vessel purchased by the Confederacy from Europe during the American Civil War was this strange looking ram ship built in France. Square-rigged and steam-driven, this clumsy iron-clad reached America too late to fight in the war and was eventually sold to Japan by the US government when hostilities ceased.

RIVER DART PADDLE STEAMER

Like many Devonshire rivers, the Dart is a flooded valley created during the Neolithic age. In 1852 there was a pilot service tug made of wood used on the Dart but shortly after an iron-built paddle steamer made especially for the ferry service was introduced called the 'Newcomin'. Later in 1865 another new iron paddler replaced her, the 'Eclair', which could carry up to 300 passengers. The 'Compton Castle' illustrated here, built by Cox & Co. near the turn of the century was one of many such craft used for pleasure and trade on the famous river. Her weight was 97 tons, 52 tons nett, 108ft. long with an 18ft. beam. This vessel now lies in a permanent mooring in Kingsbridge, serving as a museum and cafe.

AMERICAN SIDE WHEELER 1861

In the American Civil War both sides were short of vessels of war. The Union navy was inadequate and the Southern States navy consisted of a few revenue cutters, other merchant ships and southern born officers who had resigned from the US Navy. The Confederacy realised they would be blockaded and the Union felt vulnerable to attack of their large merchant fleet by Confederate raiders, one of which is illustrated, the CSS 'Nashville', a side wheeler or paddle steamer.

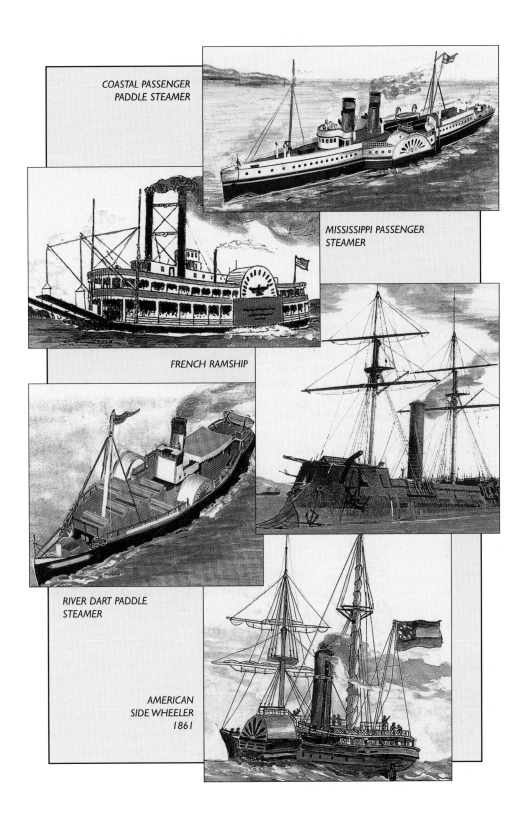

COASTAL PASSENGER
PADDLE STEAMER

MISSISSIPPI PASSENGER
STEAMER

FRENCH RAMSHIP

RIVER DART PADDLE
STEAMER

AMERICAN
SIDE WHEELER
1861

FIRST ATLANTIC CROSSING EAST TO WEST

THE 'SIRIUS', STEAM SAILER

The British and North American Steam Navigation Company was anxious to be the first to cross the Atlantic using steam paddle power, east to west. They were preparing their ship, the 'British Queen', for an 1838 spring crossing but the vessel could not be completed on time so the Company chartered the 'Sirius', a cross-channel ship of 700 tons, to make the east to west journey. Leaving Cork in Ireland on 4th April 1838 with 40 passengers on board she reached New York on the 22nd April.

The trip was not without adventure. She had to burn cabin furniture, spare yards and one of her masts to keep up steam in the final stages of the crossing. Her average speed on the trip was 6.7 knots.

The 'Great Western' arrived in New York a few hours later having left Bristol four days after the departure of the 'Sirius' from Ireland. Other ships followed owned by the British and American Company; one of these was the 'Acadia' in 1840.

STERN-WHEEL RIVER STEAMER

This type of stern-wheeler could be seen operating on many famous rivers. The Niger, Nile, St. Lawrence, Yangtze and the Mississippi all had passenger vessels of this type. Most had three deck accommodation that included long distance quarters. The rear paddle, which stretched across the stern, was driven by steam and operated by crank rods from twin steam cylinders.

HARBOUR PASSENGER TENDER

Passenger tenders, screw-driven, were a feature of many ports in Britain. They were powerful little steamers, well-fendered like harbour tugs for the work they did; performing trips to ships at anchor or taking passengers on short trips, acting as a ferry and on occasions performing as light tugs.

HARBOUR PASSENGER TENDER

*THE 'SIRIUS',
STEAM SAILER*

*AMERICAN
STERN WHEELER
1861*

SECOND CLASS TORPEDO BOAT 1880

This early torpedo boat, driven by steam, was commissioned as early as 1880. This new type of war boat was armed with a light gun and carried two torpedoes on each side in cradles released by special dropping gear. Bow tubes were later developed. This small vessel could still be found in the world's smaller navies until the late 1930s.

MISSISSIPPI TOWBOAT

Although called a towboat, the vessel was fitted with strong towing knees forward so that barges, sometimes as many as six at a time, could be pushed forward. This beamy, shallow-draught boat driven by a twin screw steam engine was capable of shifting as much as 10,000 tons of cargo weight on barges. Some vessels were stern-wheelers. Crew sizes varied depending on the size of the boat between 15 and 30 men.

NORTH SEA TRAWLER

The original North Sea steam trawler was a small craft barely 100ft. long with a 23ft. beam, made sometimes of wood and later steel. Engine power was approximately 50-60 horsepower. Sailing trawlers could only operate at a trawl depth of around 30 to 40 fathoms; the steam trawler with its controllable speed and power could increase this depth considerably. Sorting fish was done on deck after a trawl; portable divisions on deck helped to keep fish types separate before placing in the sub-divided hold below where salting and sometimes icing took place.

OCEAN TUG

Before the advent of steam, towing and tugging was a time-consuming business. Manoeuvring ships in harbour or at sea was done in a number of ways using ships' deck winches, harbour-side winches, oared boats and small amounts of sail. The steam tug with its controllable power and strength would be called upon to carry out many different tasks, as they are today. Salvage, ocean towing and harbour work were just a few jobs this small steamer could undertake. Modern tugs by comparison would dwarf these early working steamers.

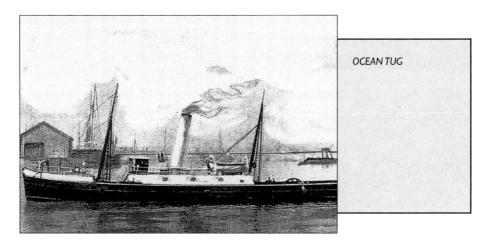

OCEAN TUG

SECOND CLASS
TORPEDO BOAT
1880

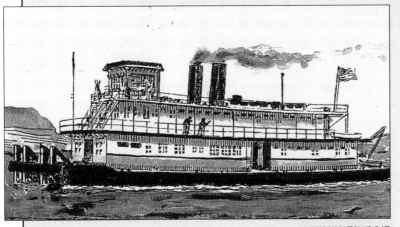

MISSISSIPPI TOWBOAT

NORTH SEA
TRAWLER

PADDLE TUG 19TH CENTURY

These useful steam-driven craft were introduced whilst sailing ships were the main type of commercial vessel. Large ships could now be moved and turned in harbour where before this task took time and much physical effort. Vessels lashed alongside the tug, rapidly turning on one paddle, could be moved in confined spaces.

RHINE TUG

Tugs on the Rhine in Germany were distinctive-looking vessels. Long low craft with widely-spaced funnels, they usually carried large anchors. Most were steam-driven paddle steamers but later diesel-driven screw vessels. The Rhine has always been a major water route for huge motor-driven and dumb barges far larger than those seen in England.

TURRET SHIP

This strange warship was introduced during the latter half of the 19th century. The guns were mounted in revolving turrets positioned on the lower deck where the bulwark portion of the gun deck is left open on both sides of the hull. The position of the twin turrets on the hull's centre line gave a low freeboard to this position. A ship of 7,790 tons launched for the British Navy in 1869 had an armoured iron hull, teak deck protected with plating and top speed of 14 knots under steam and sail.

CARGO TURRET STEAMER

The turret steamer was designed at the turn of the century to avoid the problem of shifting cargoes like rice, grain and coal. The ship side curved outwards then turned into the horizontal portion known as the 'harbour deck'. The plating then swept up to form the sides of the 'turret' with navigation platform or bridge above. Any vacant space that occured in the main lower holds was automatically filled up by the similar cargo held above in the upper hold if the cargo shifts. Other similar types were known as 'trunk-deck' steamers.

CARGO TURRET
STEAMER

PADDLE TUG
19TH CENTURY

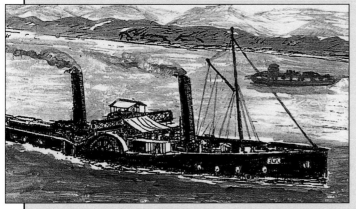

RHINE TUG

TURRET SHIP

HMS 'WARRIOR'

One of the first British iron-clad ships classified as a frigate because of her single gun deck and regarded as the world's first battleship. It was built at the Thames Iron Works, Blackwall in 1861 as a 3rd class armoured screw battleship. She was the most powerfully armed ship of the time: twenty-six 68-pounder muzzleloaders, ten 110-pounder breechloaders and four 70-pounder breechloaders and other smaller calibre guns. She formed part of the Channel Fleet in the late 1800s. It had a hull 418ft. long x 58ft.4in. beam and 9,137 tons displacement.

The photo illustration shows HMS 'Warrior' returning to Portsmouth, now her permanent moorings, after her modern refit in Hartlepool. The sailing companion is HMS 'Arrow'.

RUSSIAN WARSHIP

The 'Admiral Popov' built at Nicolaev in 1875 to the design of Vice Admiral Popov was made to provide a steady platform for large naval guns, in this case two 12in. mounted in a rotating barbette. Eight engines driving 6 propellers powered the ship of 3,553 tons. A second ship was built to this design called the 'Novgorod'. These revolutionary vessels suffered from various drawbacks, they became awash in a seaway and their flat bottoms pounded rather badly. They also became unmanageable coming downstream, revolving continuously.

Alexander II of Russia thought a round vessel a novel idea and John Elder and Company in Scotland built a royal yacht of this shape in 1880 called the 'Livadia'.

ROYAL YACHT 1899

The kings and queens of Europe have used royal yachts since the 17th century. Vessels vary in size and are used mainly for important state visits both on civil and political occasions. The largest yacht was built in Britain in 1899. She had a speed of 20 knots and a tonnage of 4,700.

ROYAL YACHT
1899

C.O.I.

H.M.S. 'WARRIOR'
AFTER REFIT

HMS 'WARRIOR'
IN PORTSMOUTH TODAY

RUSSIAN WARSHIP

SHIPS' BOATS

There is a certain basic beauty in the lines of these small boats. There must be something about their good lines of design and seaworthiness to have stood the test of time, for they changed very little over the years. These boats, especially the larger ones, were extremely versatile, being used for towing the mother ship caught in the doldrums, mounting small calibre cannons on cutting-out expeditions and making epic journeys over thousands of miles like Captain Bligh of Mutiny on the Bounty fame.

They sported many different sailing rigs when conditions were suitable as sails gave the crew a rest from rowing over longer distances.

Launch

The launch was usually the largest ships boat (as it is today). There were usually two of these, the smaller known as the Captain's barge, the larger one known as the longboat in the 18th and 19th centuries. Carvel-built with mast and sails for short sea expeditions was usual. Pulling 12 or 14 oars, double-banked, they could also accommodate a ship's cannon in the bows.

Its principal use to the ship was the transporting of heavy stores, shore-to-ship and the carting of water casks ashore for fresh water on long sea journeys. As the principal ship's boat it also served as the main lifeboat. Dry provisions and a water cask were permanently stored on board.

The developed version of the launch became the major warship's boat in the 19th and 20th centuries. Its size varied widely between 26 and 32ft. long.

Cutters

A clincher-built ship's boat measuring 24-32ft. long, pulling 8 to 14 oars depending on size. It can be rigged with two masts and lugsails. This was a much faster boat than the launch. To save space on old warships they were stowed inside the launches - there were usually two.

Pinnace

On average the pinnace was slightly smaller than the boats described above. In Nelson's time this type was hung on davits for immediate launching. Eighteen feet long was a useful size. Originally it was used with 8 oars but later increased in length to use 16 oars. One of its uses was carrying messages between ships whilst in convoy. The larger pinnace could step a mast when required and set a sloop rig.

Whaler

This boat was sharp both ends and again hung on davits. The design was taken from the original whaling boat tender with an average size around 18ft pulling oars. Yawl-rigged with triangular jib and mizzen with gunter mainsail.

The first whaler was on the port side rear davit, with the second whaler on rater ships hung on stern davits, which was sometimes called the Captain's gig.

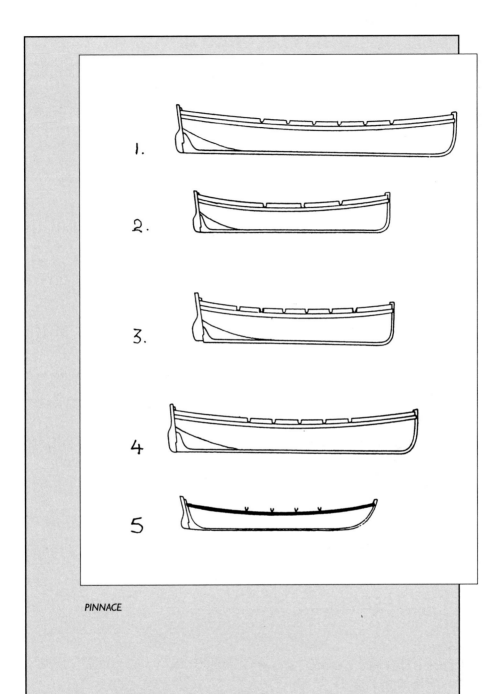

1.

2.

3.

4

5

PINNACE

Yawl

A clinker-built, robust ships boat pulling 6 oars. Yawl was a term used in the 19th century and describes the position of masts rather than a particular rig of sails. Any boat with mainmast, cutter-rigged and a mizzen stepped well back or abaft the rudder was termed yawl.

The above descriptions of the five main types of ships' boats are those found on period warships. Small types were certainly used like dinghies, skiffs and other small pulling boats. Large commercial sailers and square-rigged vessels copied the naval boats in most cases.

Lifeboat

This illustration names the parts of a common lugsail, these are much the same for all shapes of sail. Some of the named parts of the lifeboat are common to other vessels also.

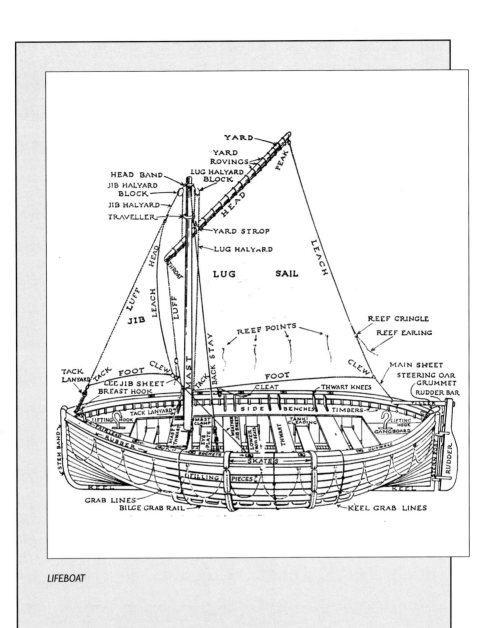

LIFEBOAT

TRADITIONAL RIGS & HULL TYPES

Some of the western traditional rigs described in this book are illustrated in the figure opposite. They are mainly those used on the majority of vessels before the 1900s. You will see them used today in some of the traditional craft used by enthusiasts, either on old salvaged vessels or those vessels reproduced as sail training ships and tall ships that race annually.

The following illustrations give details of the type and names of sail masts and yards that go to make up the rigs of square and fore-and-aft sailing vessels featured in this book.

A.	Main topgallant mast		K.	Fore topmast yard
B.	Fore topgallant mast		L.	Mizzen crossjack yard
C.	Mizzen topmast		M.	Main mast yard
D.	Main topmast		N.	Foremast yard
E.	Fore topmast		O.	Mizzen gaff
F.	Mizzen mast		P.	Mizzen boom
G.	Main mast		Q.	Bowsprit
H.	Main foremast		R.	Jib boom
I.	Mizzen topmast yard		S.	Main topgallant yard
J.	Main topmast yard		T.	Fore topgallant yard

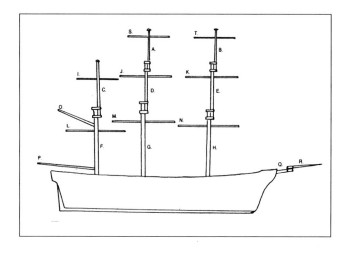

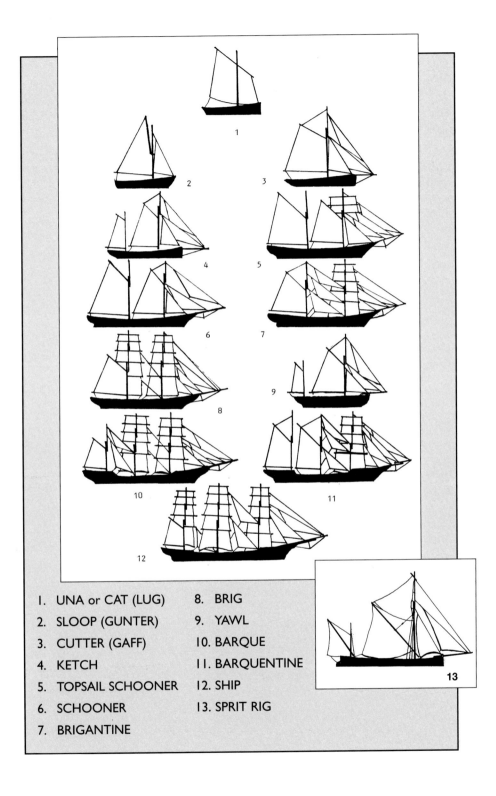

1. UNA or CAT (LUG)
2. SLOOP (GUNTER)
3. CUTTER (GAFF)
4. KETCH
5. TOPSAIL SCHOONER
6. SCHOONER
7. BRIGANTINE
8. BRIG
9. YAWL
10. BARQUE
11. BARQUENTINE
12. SHIP
13. SPRIT RIG

HULL VARIATIONS

The side view outline of a vessel can very often give an indication of the type, as the following outline drawings will show.

Decks

A.   Flush decked

B.   Mid island decked

C.   Fore and poop decked

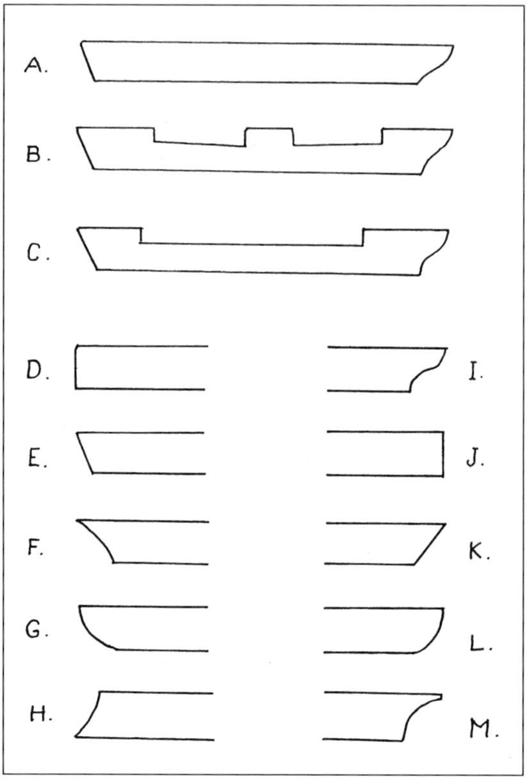

Bows

D.   Straight or vertical bow

E.   Raked bow

F.   Clipper bow

G.   Cutter bow

H.   Ram bow

Sterns

I.   Counter stern

J.   Straight or vertical transom stern

K.   Raked transom stern

L.   Spoon stern

M.   Lute stern

A. SQUARE SAIL
B. MIZZEN SPANKER
C. JIB SAIL
D. MIZZEN TOPSAIL

E. STAYSAIL
F. LATEEN SAIL
G. SPRITE SAIL
H. ARAB DHOW SAIL

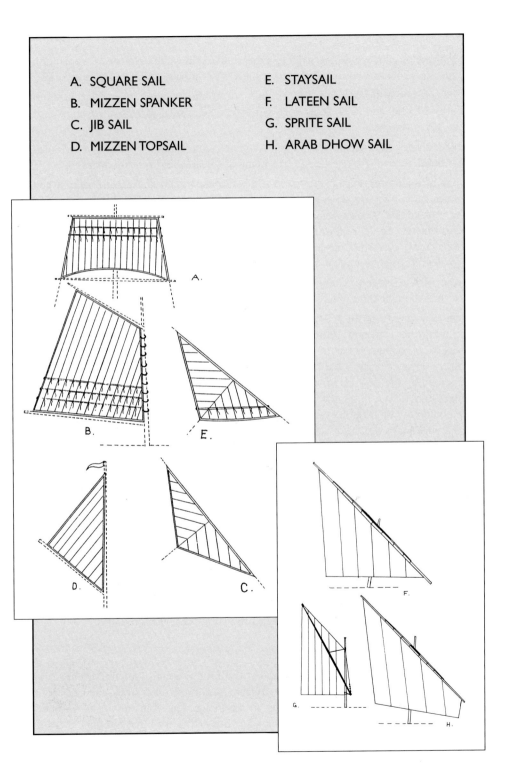

SHIPS' ORDNANCE

In England ships guns were first fitted to Edward III's ship when he made an expedition to France in 1346. It is recorded that two ships were supplied with cannons in 1358.

The Moors and Venetians are said to have used cannons on their ships in naval campaigns of 1350 and 1377. These early guns were quite small in bore, throwing a shot of 2 to 3lb. in weight.

By 1488 there were ships carrying 180 guns each. Most of these were called 'Serpentines', throwing a one-pound ball, many of these were breech-loaders.

The size of weapons gradually increased and by the early part of the 16th century gun portholes came into use. By the mid 1500s large 8in. breech-loaders were in use and by the time of the Spanish Armada, men-of-war ships had a very varied collection of ships' ordnance. Some very quaint names were given to these guns. For instance, 'cannons royal', 'culverins', 'basilisks', 'sacars', 'minions', 'falconet', 'robinets', 'port pieces' and 'fowlers' to mention a few of over twenty varieties in use.

On one of Christopher Columbus' ships, the 'Nina', during his "Enterprise of the Indies", it is thought she carried 10 early breech-loading swivel guns called 'bombardas'.

To give an example of the many sizes of shot that could be fired from smooth-bore guns during the 15th and 16th centuries, a 'whole' cannon fired a ball of 70lbs. and 'smeriglio' or 'robinets' a ball of 1/2lb. and 1lb. There were of course pieces that would fire all the intermediary sizes. The standard ship's 32lb. and 12lb. cannon and mortar were joined by the new carronade in 1779, this was a 68-pounder. Being shorter and weighing only a little more than a 12lb. ship's gun with a bore almost twice the size, these could now be fitted to the smaller ships.

Later in 1861 HMS 'Warrior', the first British iron-clad ship, a 3rd class armoured screw battleship, was armed with twenty-six 68-pounder muzzle loaders, ten 110-pounder breech loaders and four 70-pounder breech loaders.

The sizes and enormous weight of guns has had a lot to do with the size and shape of naval ships over the centuries as this brief note shows.

A)

The standard British ships' guns of the 17th, 18th and 19th century were of various calibres and barrel lengths firing balls of 32, 24, 18 and 12 pound. Originally made in bronze with techniques developed by bell founders, these guns were later made of cast iron. The average weight of a 32lb gun with wooden carriage would have been 3 tons or more. In 1805 the long 12lb gun gave way to the larger calibre carronades.

B)

The carronade was introduced in 1779 and at this time was only mounted on forecastle and poop decks but around 1805 they were used more extensively, particularly in small ships where their short length was an advantage. The 68lb carronade weighed only a little more than the original 12lb ship's gun but with a bore that was almost twice

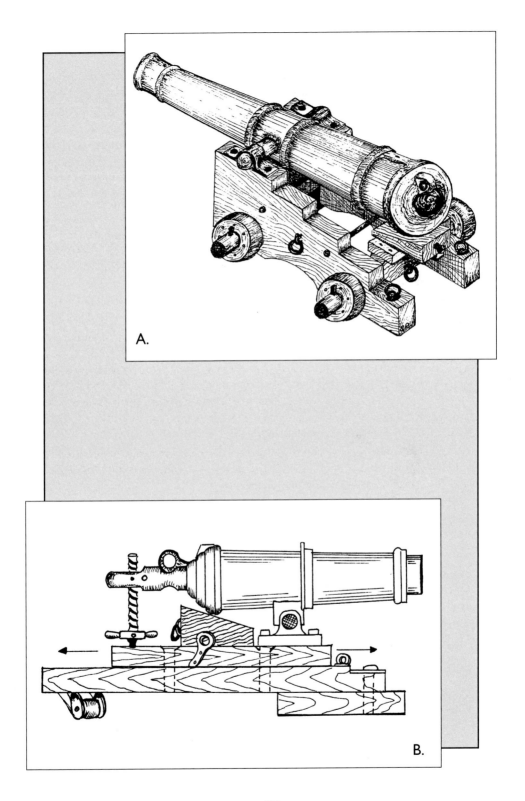

A.

B.

the size. The old quoin block used for elevating the barrel was replaced with screw-type elevation and wedge.

Ships' guns remained much the same until the early ironclad ships of 1860 when breech-loaders were being introduced.

NAVAL SHIPS COLOURS

Around the early 1800s naval hulls were black with yellow ochre bands, as HMS 'Victory'. The insides on gun decks were painted red originally, but later light yellow ochre or broken white was used. Shortly after 1815 dark soft greens began to be used for interiors and the external yellow ochre bands became white as did the interior bulkheads etc. towards the end of the century.

HMS VICTORY IN HER PERMANENT MOORINGS AT PORTSMOUTH, ENGLAND. THE STERN VIEW ILLUSTRATES WELL THE POSITION OF THE DAVITS USED FOR THE SHIP'S BOATS NEAR THE MIZZEN MASTS. A STANDARD PATTERN NAVAL GUN STANDS ON PAINTED CARRIAGE IN FORE-GROUND. THE SIDE VIEW SHOWS THE GUN PORTS OF THIS 1ST RATER'S THREE GUN DECKS

GLOSSARY OF TERMS

Aback	When the surfaces of the sail press against the mast.
Abaft	The afterpart, the stern, or on the after-side of a ship.
About	On the other tack in sailing.
A-box	The yards are said to be 'a-box' when they are braced in opposite directions.
Athwartships	At right angles to the keel.
Beam	Breadth of ship at widest point.
Bear-up	To keep farther away from the wind.
Belaying pins	These were made of wood or iron, truncheon-shaped, tapering from from the middle downwards and swelling towards the top. These push into into racks, usually at chest height. The racks were joined to the inside of the bulwarks, slightly abaft each mast. Used for belaying light ropes.
Bilge	That part of the bottom of a ship's hull nearest the keel.
Bitts	Usually a frame of two upright timbers with a cross-piece fastened horizontally near the head of uprights. Made of heavy square timber they were used to belay ropes and cables. Fore-gear and topsail sheet bitts are situated on the foredeck and round foremast. Other bitts are situated on different parts of the deck all of varying weights, depending on the degree of strength needed.
Blocks	Made usually of wood consisting of two cheeks holding a pulley wheel (sheave) made of bronze or lignum vitae. Their use in ships was to increase mechanically the power of ropes. By threading multiple and single pulleys together various haul strengths are made.
Bluff bows	Very rounded bows of some ships.
Bolster	A piece of wood usually with a rounded edge fixed to the trestletree frame to prevent the chafing of the shroud lines around the mast.
Bolt rope	A rope sewn to the edges of sails to finish and strengthen.
Bonnet	An additional strip of sail that can be laced to the foot of main course or fore-and-aft sails to increase their driving efficiency.
Boom	A spar at the foot of the main fore-and-aft sail. Minor booms were used to extend the square sail, these were attached to the main yards and called studding sail booms.
Bowsprit	Stepped into or onto the bow, supported by shroud lines, bobstay and martingale lines, it supports the headsails of a ship.
Braces	Attached to the ends of the yardarm to brace the sail around and trim the yard to the wind.

Bulkhead	A vertical partition athwartships, also for divisions fore and aft.
Bulwark	The planking or woodwork wall along the side of a ship above the deck line.
Buttock	The breadth of ship where the hull rounds down to the stern.
Caboose	American term for small deck house.
Caps	Thick blocks of wood (later caps made of iron or steel) with two holes in them, used to confine the masts at the top end of the doubling area of mast. The space between the holes allowed room for the shroud ropes to pass between the two mast sections.
Chainplates	Thick iron rods or straps bolted to the sides of ships to which chains or shackles connect to the lower deadeye that support the masts' shrouds.
Carvel-built	A type of side planking where the edges are fitted tightly together making a smooth finish. The joints are caulked.
Channels	Broad thick planks bolted edgeways against the ship's side through which the chainplates pass. This spaces the shrouds from each other.
Cheeks or bibbs	Pieces of timber bolted to the mast on either side of a square-rigged ship to support the trestletrees.
Cleats	Blocks of wood or metal shaped in various ways to belay ropes and lines
Clinker-built (also clincher-built)	A method of planking in which the lower edge of each plank overlaps the upper edge on the one below. A method normally used in small boat building.
Con	To con a ship is to direct her steering.
Counter stern	The overhang of the stern abaft the rudder.
Course	The largest sails set upon all lower yards of a square-rigged ship, referred to as fore course, main course etc.
Crab winch	A hand winch positioned aft on either side of a barge, used to raise and lower lee-boards etc.
Cringles	Small rope loops on the sail bolt rope used to fasten different ropes including the leech rope.
Crosstrees (1)	Part of the wooded frame running athwart of the mast that supports the tops.
Crosstrees (2)	The word is sometimes used to describe both trestletrees and crosstrees which form a frame around the top mast and is left unboarded in this case.
Crotches	Pieces of iron or wood shaped with a broad 'U' shaped top. They are usually mounted at deck level to support spare masts and yard timber.

Deadeyes	Wooden blocks, circular with flattened sides, pierced with three holes. A rope groove cut around the periphery. Used to reeve lanyards when setting up shrouds or stays.
Davit	A stout boom fitted to the fore-channel, used to assist the lifting of the anchor keeping it clear of the ship's side. A kind of crane hoist, hinged on the channel. Also used to raise and lower the ship's boats situated on the mizzen channels both sides. On the stern the Captain's gig was lowered on two davit arms permanently bolted in a horizontal position, projecting over the stern.
Eye of a shroud	The top end of a shroud formed into a served loop to go over the mast head.
Fid	A large wooden or iron wedge that goes through the heel of the topmast. The fid rests on the trestletrees preventing the mast dropping through.
Fife rail	A sturdy perforated rail supported by two vertical timbers positioned at the base of the mast for belaying ropes from above to belaying pins.
Flushdeck	When the deck is the same height from the water throughout its length.
Forecastle deck	Pronounced fo'c'sle - the forward deck and underpart.
Foremast	The first mast mounted nearest to the bows of a square-rigged ship.
Freeboard	The distance, measured in the centre of the ship, from waterline to deck level.
Frigate	A class of three-masted warship, fully rigged on each mast. Armed with from 24 to 38 guns carried on a single gun deck. Rated 5th or 6th rate.
Futtock shroud	The section of the shroud lines from the underside of the top that connect with the mast band in some cases, or the lower mast shrouds in others.
Gaffs	A spar to which the head of a four-sided fore-and-aft sail is laced and hoisted on the after side of the mast.
Gammon lashing	A rope lashing consisting of seven or eight turns passing or gammoning over the bowsprit and through a slot or hole in the stem. This was usually a cross lashing. Later in the 19th century it was replaced by a heavy metal band.
Gunwales	The plank that covers the head of the timbers around the upper sheer strake of a ship.
Halyards, Halliards or Haulyards	The cables or ropes used to hoist or lower sails and their yards. The heavy course sails (lowest sail on square-rigged ships) were hoisted by jeers from just under the tops.

Hammock netting	A stowage place for hammocks (bedding rolls of sailors). Old sailing warships had iron frames bolted to the sides of the centre section of deck and upper deck and along the break of the poop to act as protection from musket fire and wood splinters during battle. Capital ships had eight hundred odd men as crew so there were plenty of hammock rolls.
Hatch coamings	Sturdy boards mounted vertically around deck openings like cargo hatches to prevent water running down into the openings. These were six to ten inches high in sailing ships with good freeboard but higher on seagoing barges.
Horses	The rope that sailors stood on, slung under the yards of a square-rigged sail, when furling sails. A bowsprit horse runs parallel from the bowsprit and serves as a rail hold or foot rope for sailors going out on the bowsprit. Jib horses hang under the jib boom and are knotted into a course net as a safety foot net.
Hounds	Wooden shoulders bolted below the masthead either side of some ships without trestletrees to support the shroud top.
Hull	Body of the ship.
Jeers	Heavy tackle consisting of double or treble blocks used for hoisting the lower yards in square-rigged ships. A jeer capstan was usually situated between fore and main masts to sway up the yards.
Jib boom	This was an overlapped extension of the bowsprit held by a cap and band. This supported the fore topgallant and royal headstays and sails.
Jury mast	A temporary mast fitted in place of one broken or carried away.
Keel	The lowest and principal timber of a wooden ship running fore and aft.
King plank	The centre plank of the ship's deck on wooden vessels.
King post	A short mast close to cargo hatches from which is worked small cargo derrick.
Lanyards	Short ropes threaded between deadeyes. Also to tie hearts together on main stays.
Larboard	Old term for port.
Leeboard	An early type of drop keel made of wood pivoted outboard each side of barges and other flat-bottomed or shallow-draught sailing vessels. Said to have been developed by the Dutch.
Lubber hole	A small aperture in the top for the less brave to go through rather than climbing out via the futtock shrouds to gain the top.
Lutchet	A similar fitting to the tabernacle at deck level found on spritsail barges or wherries allowing the mast to be lowered.
Luff	The leading edge of a fore-and-aft sail.

Lugsail	A four-sided sail set on a lug or yard, used mainly in small craft.
Main mast	The centre mast of a square-rigged sailing ship.
Martingale	A bar of wood, usually ash, projecting downwards from the underside of the bowsprit cap. The martingale stay supports the jib boom.
Mast	A vertical spar set in a ship's deck to support other spars that in turn support the sails.
Mast butt	The thick end of a mast nearest the keel, or thick end of masts above the lower mast.
Mizzen mast	The name of the third, aftermost mast of a square-rigged ship.
Mule rigged	'Mulie' mizzens, as on barges, consisted of a standard mizzen mast with conventional gaff and booms, as opposed to a sprit mizzen.
Parral	A method of keeping a yard against the mast and to facilitate the swing, raising and lowering of the yard. Wooden trucks threaded on wooden ribs lashed around the mast.
Poop deck	The stern or quarter deck.
Quoin	A large wooden wedge used under the butt end of naval cannons to obtain elevation. Superseded later by various fast thread screws mounted to the gun.
Rake	The inclination of a mast from the perpendicular.
Ratlings or Ratlines	Small ropes that cross the shrouds horizontally at equal distances, forming a ladder to go up or down from the deck to masthead.
Running rigging	Ropes and cordage, usually running on pulley blocks that control the sails and spars of sailing ships.
Shallop	Originally the largest or second largest rowing or sailing ship's boat. In England the name was dropped and the term longboat was used from the 17th century onwards although the term was still used in Europe up to the 1800s.
Scuppers	These were draining holes or slots cut into the base of the deck bulwarks to drain surface water from the decks and waterways.
Sheave	The revolving wheel in a block. Made of lignum vitae or bronze.
Sheer	Upward curve of deck towards bows and stern.
Sheets	Any rope that controls a sail from its lower corners.
Ship draft	Shipwright's plans of ship.
Shipwrights	The ship-building experts.
Shrouds	A variety of large ropes from the mastheads down to the sides of the ship i.e. fore, main and mizzen shrouds. This also applies to the topmast shrouds. The bowsprit also has shrouds that support it.

Sloop	This term was used to describe several different types of vessel. In Europe it originally described a single masted vessel with a single head sail; all fore and aft, as in some cutters of the period. In America it described similar vessel setting two head sails. It was used over a long period for auxiliary naval vessels and in the 18th century it loosely described those naval vessels that had no recognised class as minor war ships. By the start of the 19th century it described two types of war vessel, a ship sloop three masts, a brig sloop two masts, all squared rigged on all masts.
Snotter	Metal gear found on sprit-rigged vessels consisting of a ring collar which fits over the heel of the sprit boom. It is chain-linked to the metal main mast strap. This supports the sprit boom, holding it close to the mast.
Soldier's wind	A wind that will allow a boat to reach its destination without having to tack.
Spar	General term for timbers used in setting up the rigging and sails.
Spritsail	A large fore-and-aft four-sided sail set on a sprit spar which stretched diagonally across the sail to support the peak. A typical barge rig. The name also describes a small square sail set on a yard beneath the bowsprit in a square-rigged ship, introduced in the 16th century.
Standing rig	Stout rigging ropes which are permanently set up to support the masts of sailing ships, as in the shrouds.
Stay	Part of the standing-rigging of a sailing vessel which supports a mast in the fore-and-aft line. Fore-stays support forward and backstays from aft.
Steerage way	When a ship has sufficient speed for the rudder to act efficiently.
Stem	The foremost timber of a ship. It is attached to the keel.
Sternpost	The aftermost timber in the hull. It is attached to the keel and forms a fixing for the rudder.
Strakes	Each line of planking in a wooden ship.
Swimhead bow	Early type of barge bow, not unlike the wedge-shaped punt bow superseded by the straight stem bow.
Tabernacle	A wooden or metal trunk fitted to the deck of sailing ships supporting the heel of a mast, stepped at deck level. A fitting usually found on vessels that have to lower masts under bridges.
Tack	When a ship changes direction with the rudder, using the wind on the opposite quarter.
Throat	The inner end of a gaff or boom.
Timberheads	Vertical timbers rising through deck affording fixings for bulwark planking.
Tops	The platform structure fixed around the head of the lower mast that rests on the crosstrees.

Transom	Stern bulkhead. The squared-off stern: sometimes vertical, often canted at an angle.
Trestletrees	Part of the wooded frame, running fore-and-aft of the mast that supports the tops.
Truck	A circular wooden cap with small sheaves fitted to the tops of masts. It was used for signal flags. It can also refer to the wooden wheels of a gun carriage.
Tuck	The shape of the afterbody of a ship under the stern or counter. The light fir-planked frigates built towards the end of the Napoleonic Wars (1803-15) had flat square transoms. They were known as square-tucked frigates.
Tumble home	The amount by which the two sides of a ship are brought in towards the centreline after reaching their maximum beam.
Vang	The two ropes leading from the outer end of a gaff in fore-and-aft sails to prevent leeward sagging of sail and give more control over gaff.
Wales	An extra thickness of wood bolted to the sides of ships in positions where protection is needed.
Wind rode	When at anchor a ship rides by force of wind instead of tide.
Yards	A large wooden spar crossing and attached to the mast horizontally to support a square sail.
Yaw	A ship is said to yaw when she is not steering a straight course

BIBLIOGRAPHY

Anderson, R.C. Seventeenth Century Rigging. Model & Allied Publications 1972.

Archibald, Michael South Eastern Sail 1840-1940. David & Charles 1972.

Beck, Stuart. Ships Boats and Craft. H. Jenkins Ltd.

Blandford, Percy. An illustrated history of Small Boats. Spurbooks Limited.

Campbell, G.F. Jackstay. Model Shipways Co. Inc. N.J.

Chapelle, H.I. American Sailing Craft. Bonanza Books N.Y.

Chapelle, H.I. The Search for Speed Under Sail. Geo. Allen & Unwin Ltd.

Chapman, F.H. Architectura Navalis Mercatoria. Adlard Coles Ltd. 1768.

Christies. Maritime Catalogue, Christies. South Kensington.

Colledge, J.J. British Sailing Warships. Ian Allan Books.

Cooper, F.S. Handbook of Sailing Barges. Adlard Coles Ltd. & John de Graff N.Y.

Corin, Cohn. Provident and the Story of Brixham Smacks.

Culver, Harry B. Contemporary Scale Models of Vessels of the Seventeenth Century. Payson & Clarke N.Y. 1926.

Davis, C.G. American Sailing Ships (Their Plans and History). Dover Pub. Ltd. N.Y.

Dorling, T. (R.N.). All About Ships. Cassell & Co. Ltd. 1912.

Dudszus, Alfred & Henriot. Ernest. Dictionary of Ship Types. Conway Maritime Press 1986.

Editors, The Civil War, Blockade Runners & Raiders. Time Life Books, Virginia.

Editors. The Civil War, The Coastal War. Time Life Books, Virginia.

Fouille, G. The Story of Ships. Hamlyn.

Frere-Cook, Gervis (Ed). The Decorative Arts of the Mariner. Jupiter 1974.

Greenhill, Basil. The Archaeology of the Boat. A & C Black, London 1976.

Greenhill, Basil & Gifford, Ann. Sailing Ships: Victorian & Edwardian from Old Photographs. Batsford Books.

Haws, Duncan. Ships and the Sea. Hart Davis, MacGibbon, London 1976.

Hazell, Martin. Sailing Barges. Shire Publications Ltd.

HMSO (Admiralty). Manual of Seamanship. HMSO 1908 (Revised 1915).

HMSO Ship Models from Earlier Times to 1700AD (1963).

Hough, Richard. Fighting Ships, Michael Joseph 1969.

Jobe, Joseph (Ed), The Great Age of Sail. Edita Lausanne 1967.

Jutsum, Capt. J.N. Knots and Splices, The Nautical Press, Glasgow 1926.

Kemp, Peter (Ed). The Oxford Companion to Ships and the Sea. Oxford University Press, London, New York and Melbourne.

Leavitt, John F. Wake of the Coasters. The American Maritime Library Vol 2. 2nd ed. 1984.

MacGregor, David. Fast Sailing Ships 1775-1875 Conway 1988.

MacGregor, David. Merchant Sailing Ships 1775-1815. Argus Books Ltd. 1980.

McKee, E. Working Boats of Britain. Conway Maritime Press 1983.

Pain Lincoln. Ships of the World. Conway Publications.

Rees, Abraham. Rees's Naval Architecture 1816-20.

Slocum, Capt. Joshua. Sailing Alone Around the World and Voyage of the Liberade. Rupert Hart-Davis 1948.

Stader, C.R. Guide to United States Military History 1815-1865. Sachem Publishing Assoc. Inc.

Steel, David. Art of Rigging 1818. Fisher Nautical Press 1974.

Traditional Sail Review. 1984 Maldon, Essex.

Van Powell, Nowland. The American Navies of the Revolutionary War. C.P. Putnam & Sons NY 1974.

Various. Art and the Seafarer. Faber & Faber 1968.

Various. The Law of Ships, Nordbook. Sweden 1975.

Veryan, Heal. Britain's Maritime Heritage (Museums & Maritime Collections). Conway Maritime Press.

Williams, Guy R. The World of Model Ships and Boats. Andre Deutsch 1971.

INDEX

SMALL SAILING SHIPS, BOATS & CRAFT

PAGE

MISCELLANEOUS DETAILS